THE GENTLE ART

of

QUILT-MAKING

THE
GENTLE
ART

of

QUILT-MAKING

15 Projects Inspired by Everyday Beauty

JANE BROCKET

PAVILION

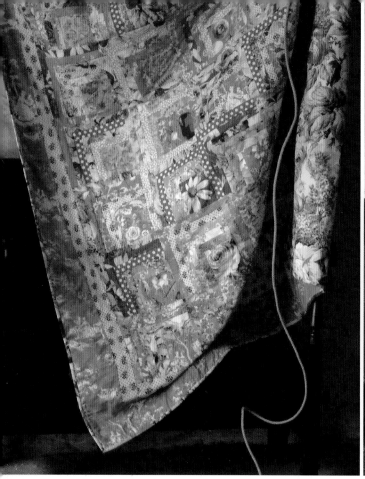

This edition published in the United Kingdom
in 2015 by
Pavilion
1 Gower Street
London
WC1E 6HD

ISBN 978-1-91090-429-9

A CIP catalogue for this book is available from
the British Library.

10 9 8 7 6 5 4 3 2 1

Reproduction by Dot Gradations Ltd., UK
Printed and bound by 1010 Printing
International Ltd, China

This book can be ordered direct from the
publisher at www.pavilionbooks.com

Dedication

For my favourite quilt users and consultants:
Simon, Tom, Alice and Phoebe

contents

Introduction

This is a book about quilt inspiration: where to find it and how to use it. It is for anyone who has ever wanted to make stunning, imaginative quilts with the minimum of fuss, no matter how basic your sewing skills or how limited you are by time and space. Far more important are enthusiasm, beautiful fabrics and a good measure of inspiration – which, as I make clear, is all around us.

My aim is to inspire trust in simplicity of design and technique, and to instil the confidence to create meaningful, personal quilts. The sixteen simple, yet effective, quilt designs here show you how to create big effects with little effort, using plenty of wonderful fabrics. Whether you are a seasoned quilter or a complete beginner, I hope that *The Gentle Art of Quilt-Making* will encourage you to make simple, vibrant quilts and to dispense with concerns about complexity, perfection, rigid designs and knowledge of special techniques.

I was inspired to make quilts long before I actually made one. I saw, admired and envied many quilts in galleries, exhibitions, books and friends' houses, but did not think that I was capable of making one of my own in a way that pleased me and gave me the results I wanted. My fear of doing things 'wrong' or in the 'incorrect way' held me back for years until I had a perception-altering conversation with my friend Lucy.

It was a cold winter's day and we were having a cup of tea by the wood-burning fire in Lucy's cosy parlour, and I was telling her how much I loved quilts and how much I wanted to make one, but that I was convinced it was all rules and regulations and that I thought it would be too difficult. 'Oh, for goodness' sake, Jane,' she said in exasperation, 'all you have to do is cut up some fabric and sew it together!'

Although she didn't realize it at the time, her throwaway wise words would stay with me – I'm especially reminded of them when I find myself on the brink of over-complicating the quilting process – and the more I thought about it, the more I knew Lucy was right. She had finally made me see that I, with my imagined difficulties, was turning something that has been done in a matter-of-fact way by people over the years into something mysteriously complicated that could only be done by a few gifted individuals. Instead, I began to adopt a can-do, simplified approach to patchwork and quilting, and as soon as I let go of the ideas of perfection and right and wrong ways of doing things, quilts were no longer a dream, but a real possibility.

The first step was to go on a weekend course at which I learned the absolute basics of cutting out fabric and sewing it back together. I learned how to use a rotary cutter, quilting rulers and a self-healing mat, how to handle fabric, how to machine-piece, bind and finish a quilt. And, crucially, I came away with a new-found confidence about the quilting process and the many, many quilting possibilities.

My first three or four quilts were experiments with my newly acquired techniques following simple designs in very clear 'how-to' books. However, I soon found myself deliberately moving away from what I call the 'jigsaw' approach (in which pieces of fabric are slotted into a frame rather like the pieces of a puzzle) to a much more colourful and personal approach that expresses the inspiration I find all around me, and uses beautiful fabrics rather than complicated designs to create impact.

This has been my approach ever since, and I still have not run out of inspiration or ideas, and nor am I likely ever to do so. As a result, my quilts are most definitely not heirloom quilts, but are instead practical quilts that I have enjoyed making and truly like, quilts that are warm, useful, visually pleasing and packed with thoughts and associations. This is private, personal quilt-making as an absorbing creative pastime with lovely results, rather than quilt-making for show or competition.

This book encapsulates my quilting philosophy of seeking inspiration and using it to make colourful, meaningful quilts. It is for anyone who's ever hesitated on the threshold of a fabric shop, or swooned over fabrics but not known what to do with them, and for anyone who wants quilting to be a simple, worry- and stress-free process with a significant element of enjoyment and playfulness. My aim is simplification, not complication, and I spell out in the text that accompanies each quilt how to interpret and express inspiration. In doing so, I hope to encourage anyone who so wishes to ignore the tyranny of perfection and to have a go.

I hope to reassure tentative quilters (always remembering that I once was one) that quilting is easy and incredibly enjoyable, that anyone can do it in an ordinary home environment and without a dedicated room or table or design board, and that you don't need hundreds of expensive fabrics. And I would like to convince you that, with a few fabrics and a small number of specialist tools you can create gorgeous quilts that reflect something of their maker's personality and individuality, quilts that give pleasure both in the making and the finished article. I would also be pleased to know I have inspired someone to take a few risks with colour and pattern, and to experience the excitement and pleasure of creating a simple but beautiful quilt by making individual decisions and not simply by following step-by-step instructions.

So come with me and venture into a world of colour and pattern, memories and associations, warmth and comfort and, above all, inspiration. You may find that this is a book of surprises; that every quilt tells a story, that you can do it, that basic patterns can be supremely clever (which is why they have been around for so long), that making lovely quilts is not difficult, and that the results will be something of which you can be justifiably proud.

I hope this book will inspire you to quilt just as I have been inspired to quilt by so many wonderful colours, fabrics, places, patterns, gardens, exhibitions, quilters and quilts.

Jane Brocket

every quilt tells a story

One of the great pleasures of doing anything repetitive by hand, whether it's knitting, making bread, chopping onions or sowing seeds, is that the rhythm of the action allows your mind to wander. Now some people may find that their mind just stays a blank in a kind of suspended animation, or maybe they use the time to compile their shopping lists or think about work or plan their next novel, but I know that many quilters (and stitchers and knitters) value the quiet moments of being with their hands, textiles, needles, threads and machines and enjoy letting their mind roam freely in association with what they are making.

This is how quilt stories or narratives are developed. Once you have mastered the basics of quilting (and I do keep all the basics very basic), you will find you have the confidence to relax and enjoy the processes instead of worrying about adhering to rules, complicated techniques and other complexities that can dominate the mind. If you choose to take simple, timeless and often childlike quilt patterns and frameworks, you can play with them and fill them with colour, vitality and stories. The result will be a quilt that can be enjoyed over and over again in the making, the telling and the using.

Once I had made a couple of very simple quilts, learned the basics of cutting and piecing, and overcome my nerves as I made my first tentative steps and stitches, I found it was possible to start enjoying the process, and it wasn't long before I was putting a layer of meaning into the sandwich of my quilts.

I realized that every decision I made, whether small or large, was made for a reason. I started thinking about why I liked certain fabrics and the associations they stirred in me, and why I'd decided to put them in one order rather than another, and what it all made me think of. So the Hydrangea quilt began as an 'inky' quilt because the fabrics I had put together were, I thought initially, like dark inks; but as the quilt grew, and more deep pinks and magentas crept in, they persuaded me that it was more like a quilt of hydrangeas growing in strips by walls or in borders in Brittany and Normandy.

Or instead I might take a source of inspiration and apply it to the quilt, weaving a story into the making. So the Lisbon Tile quilt is infused with memories of wandering around the city in May, noticing and admiring the incredible number and variety of the tiles. And the Floral Frocks quilt arose directly out of an exhibition I visited, which in turn brought back many memories of summer dresses.

The idea of quilt stories or narratives is as old as quilt-making itself. Quilters have always come together and told and retold stories as they stitched, and there has never been a time when individual quilters did not stitch stories, memories, hopes and wishes into their quilts. Think of quilt bees, community and collaborative quilts,

friendship quilts and wedding quilts, quilts for children who are leaving home and quilts that use old family fabrics – and the ways in which all these create textile narratives of histories, lives and places.

Investing your quilt with a story is a lovely way to feel connected both with the sources of inspiration and with the quilters of yesteryear, and it makes the process far more meaningful, personal, enjoyable and imaginative, and far removed from the 'jigsaw' approach of simply placing pieces of fabric in a preset pattern. It may also be a little more risky, but it's worth the gamble every time.

Each quilt in this book comes with a story and every time I look at one of them I am reminded of what inspired it. And that is a lovely feeling.

important note about fabric quantities

I call it relaxed, but others may call it haphazard – my personal approach to buying fabrics is far from scientific. I rarely buy all the fabrics for a quilt in one go (whether from a shop or website), as I like to collect the fabrics over a period of time and from different sources. This means that I have never been aware of the exact amounts needed for a quilt top: I simply get out the fabrics that I have collected and start from there. This method may sound chaotic, but in fact it allows for a much more enjoyable, liberated approach to putting a quilt together because I can add or take away fabrics that do or don't work, and I don't have the fear of running out of a fabric if I make a mistake.

There are several reasons for working this way, and they are based on my belief that quilts should be made with available fabrics, adapting and improvising along the way, and not be a slavish copy of a pre-set pattern. This may initially cause you jitters if you have never worked this way before, but I assure you that if you relax and let the quilt grow organically according to the fabrics and the way the burgeoning quilt looks, you will soon know when to carry on adding fabrics and when to stop.

When I started making quilts, I was terrified about making mistakes when cutting and thus wasting fabric, and I always bought more than I thought I would need. If a design stipulated a frighteningly exact amount, I could guarantee that this would make me so nervous that I would cut the fabric the wrong way and end up with a useless piece. Buying in rounded-up amounts was the best way to feel comfortable about having sufficient quantities and therefore about making a quilt, so I adopted this flexible approach to calculating fabric requirements and still always buy more than I expect to use – not a great deal, but always rounding up to the nearest half-yard or half-metre.

(I have learned that there is no such thing as wasted fabric, just fabric waiting its turn to be in a quilt or, if the pieces are really small, waiting to be turned into dolls' clothes.)

I tend not to plan too far ahead when I begin a quilt and I don't keep to standard bed sizes (i.e. UK single, double, king size). Instead, I make my quilts according to the fabrics and time available and let them grow naturally. So my quilts may end up wider or longer, narrower or shorter than commercial bedding, but this does not worry me. If you do want a quilt to fit a certain size of bed, take some measurements before you begin and consider whether you want the quilt to hang down over the sides and cover the pillow.

Here are some guideline sizes for the quilts in this book, although there is nothing to stop you enlarging or reducing any of the quilts simply by increasing or reducing the number of strips or squares or blocks:

— Quilts for double or king-size beds: Tulip Field quilt, Green, Green Grass of Home quilt (made larger), Floral Frocks quilt (made larger), Sample Book quilt.

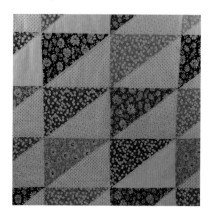

— Quilts for a single bed: Green, Green Grass of Home quilt, Lisbon Tile quilt (made larger), Hydrangea quilt, Floral Frocks quilt, Amaryllis quilt.

— Smaller quilts for use on sofas/ armchairs/ children's beds/ by the fire/ in hammocks/ keeping warm outside/ on car journeys: Russian Shawl quilt, Postage Stamp quilt, Suits and Ties quilt, Lisbon Tile quilt, Charming Chintz quilt.

Please note that the fabric quantities given for each project in this book can be increased or reduced according to the size of quilt you want to make.

quilt tops

The amount of fabric needed for the top of a quilt varies markedly according to the design, as you must always allow for a ¼in (6mm) seam allowance all around on everything you cut – so, for example, if you are planning to make a quilt with squares measuring 4in (10cm) when finished, you need to cut the fabric into 4½in (11cm) squares. It stands to reason that a quilt made up of small squares will need more fabric than one made of huge strips or squares, simply because you have to allow for all the seams. Generally speaking, though, you will need a total of 4–5 yards or metres for a quilt for a single bed, and approximately 6 yards or metres for a quilt for a double or king-size bed.

backing and binding fabrics

It's far easier to calculate accurately the amount of fabric needed to back or bind a quilt after the quilt top has been made, especially if you adopt the 'go-with-the-flow' approach to building up a quilt, which means you don't know before you start exactly what size the finished quilt will be.

I rarely buy fabric for either backing or binding before starting a quilt (see Decisions, Decisions, page 15) unless I fall in love with a design that I know without doubt would be lovely on the back of a quilt I have in mind, or I see something in a sale that I know I would happily pay full price for and so is worth buying. And now I must confess that, when this happens, I buy as many as 5–6 yards or metres, knowing that

6 yards or metres is the maximum I'll need for a quilt back, and if it turns out that I don't use it all, I'll be more than happy to use the remaining fabric in a quilt top or a binding. An example of this is the wonderful 'Lilac Rose' fabric designed by Philip Jacobs, which I use on the back of the Purple Rain quilt (see page 102). I adore this fabric and bought a whopping 6 metres, but have used it not only for the backing but also in strips in the blocks and for the binding, and I still have some left over.

To calculate backing fabric

The first thing you need to remember is that not all quilt fabrics are exactly the same width; they vary from about 41–45in (104–114cm) wide (a little less, if you pre-wash them as I do). But, like many quilters, I use 42in (106cm) as my standard width when doing calculations.

I place backing fabric to run lengthways (to give a vertical seam or seams), but it is possible to place it to run widthways (to give a horizontal seam or seams). I take the easy route and simply sew the widths together, which usually gives a seam down the centre of the back, but some people prefer not to have the seam on the place where you fold up the quilt, and prefer to cut one width into two and sew this on either side of a central width to give two seams between a central column and the two side columns. I am a little fussy about matching up the pattern on the back, and the more seams you have, the more the pattern is broken up, so I keep it very simple.

- When calculating how much backing fabric you will need, allow for it to be 3–4in (7.5–10cm) bigger all around than the quilt top, as it can be very tricky manoeuvring

fabric once it's in layers, and the chances of getting the corners and edges of the quilt top and the backing fabric perfectly aligned are virtually nil.

- If you are planning to get someone to machine-quilt the quilt using a long-arm quilter, you need to make the backing 4in (10cm) bigger all around than the quilt top.

- If the fabric is plain or has a very small repeat pattern (e.g. polka dots), you do not need to worry about matching the seams on the backing exactly. If the fabric has a large repeat (e.g. the 'Lilac Rose' fabric on page 102), you will need to allow extra fabric to accommodate the matching of the pattern across the back (unless, of course, it does not bother you if it is mismatched).

— Make the calculation by taking the length of the quilt plus the extra allowance and dividing that by 36in if working in yards, and 100cm if working in metres, to get the amount of fabric needed for one length of backing. Double or treble this according to the width of the quilt and the backing fabric; quilts up to 74in (188cm) wide will need two full widths. For example, for a quilt 72in (183cm) long and 60in (152cm) wide, to be backed with a spotty or stripy or small repeat design, you'll need 72in (183cm) + 8in (20cm) = 80in (203cm) x 2 widths = 160in (406cm) in total, which I would round up to 4½ yards or metres.

— If there is a large repeat, you need to add the size of this to the calculation. For example, for a quilt 72in (183cm) long and 60in (152cm) wide, to be backed with a fabric with a 10in (25cm) repeat, you'll need eight repeats per width, plus the excess, so 80in (203cm) + 8in (20cm) = 88in (223cm) x 2 = 176in (446cm) in total, which I'd round up to 5 yards or metres.

— Finally, if the width of the quilt exceeds two full widths of backing fabric, or you haven't got quite enough fabric going lengthways and you are reluctant to buy another width simply for the sake of a few inches, you can use a strip of contrasting fabric or fabrics at one side or at the top or bottom of the backing. I do this regularly; it adds interest to the back and uses up smaller pieces of fabric from my collection (see Tulip Fields, Green, Green Grass of Home quilts).

To calculate binding fabric

It's simpler to calculate binding fabric. Normally I use a single fabric, but sometimes I make a long strip out of leftovers from the quilt. I work with strips 2½in (6cm) wide, folded double; some quilters like to use 2¼in (5.75cm) strips, but I find this doesn't always quite cover mistakes or less-than-straight stitching.

— To work out the length of strip you need to go all the way round the quilt, measure the full perimeter of the quilt (i.e. top, bottom and two sides), and add an extra allowance of 6–8in (15–20cm). For example, with a quilt 60 x 72in (152 x 183cm), multiply 60in (152cm) by 2 and 72in (183cm) by 2, then add together to get 264in (670cm). With the extra 12in (30cm) allowance, the total comes to 276in (700cm).

— Divide the outside edge measurement plus allowance by 42in (106cm) – the average width of a pre-washed quilt fabric, but if your fabric is narrower then it's important you put this width into the calculation – to give the number of strips needed, i.e. 276in (700cm) divided by 42in (106cm) = 6.6, so you'll need to cut seven strips.

— Multiply the number of strips by the width of the strips, in this case 2½in (6cm), to find out how much fabric you require. So seven strips x 2½in (6cm) wide = 17½in (42cm), which can be rounded up to 20in (50cm) to allow for shrinkage when pre-washing.

decisions, decisions

It's very easy to rush headlong into quilting and to get caught up in a whirlwind of making. However, it's also very easy to become paralysed by the challenge of translating inspiration and a pile of fabrics into a finished quilt. So it helps, in both cases, to take a deep breath and to take quilt-making one step at a time.

I was very apprehensive when I first started quilting until I took a weekend course and learned the basic skills of using a rotary cutter, self-healing mat and quilter's ruler, and discovered that these were all I needed in order to make the sorts of quilts I wanted to make (the sort you see here in this book). There are plenty more techniques I can (and may yet) acquire, but I found that once I was confident with cutting and handling fabric, I could deal with the elements of making a quilt in a step-by-step fashion, rather than sticking doggedly to a vision of what I was aiming to achieve. The more quilts I made, the more I broke down quilt-making into a series of decisions, something that makes the whole process far more enjoyable and far less nerve-racking.

This section explains how the decision-making process works so that quilt-making becomes an enjoyable, creative, worry-free experience with a significant element of pleasure and playfulness.

choosing and buying fabric

The first things you need are inspiration and fabric. I talk about inspiration elsewhere in this book, so will concentrate on fabric here. You may be inspired by an idea, a visual, a pattern or design, or a specific fabric, and once you have the spark or the idea (which may come from a fabric), you need to gather together the fabrics for your quilt.

Deciding which fabrics to buy is a very personal thing and best done when you have time to browse, consider, reconsider, build up piles of bolts of cloth and play with combinations. This is the beauty of browsing on the Internet: it's very easy to fill a shopping basket, take a break and come back to review your selection. It's not always as easy in a busy shop, where you feel you might be disturbing the arrangements and taking too long, but don't rush – these places are used to customers making thoughtful, time-consuming purchases (and if you do feel uncomfortable, then shame on the shop). It's worth asking for a second opinion, too, to help you decide; quilt shop staff are usually experienced quilters who may be able to make excellent suggestions.

I rarely decide to buy all the fabric I need for a quilt in one shopping expedition (an exception is the Ball Gown quilt on page 82). I have found that it's too easy to get carried away with a theme and the convenience of a single-stop shopping expedition, and have sometimes come home with fabrics I really wish I hadn't bought. Check what you've got at home before you set off (or rummage and check your stocks while you are online), keep an open mind, shop around if necessary and take your time. Your quilt will be all the better for a little extra consideration.

The best way to make good, true decisions is to go browsing when you are looking for nothing in particular and therefore not under pressure. This is when the fabrics you truly love catch your eye and seduce you, and you know immediately that you want to make a quilt with them. This is when you need to trust your instincts; I regret very few impulse purchases of stunning fabrics I have found when not looking for anything specific, because I have bought them for all the right reasons and subsequently loved using them.

And now there is the vexed question of how much to buy. I buy everything in half- or full yards or metres, and if I really, really love something I buy two yards or metres of it. This may seem extravagant, but as I don't have a very big collection of fabrics (not by some quilters' standards), I don't mind having leftovers that can then go into another project (if I liked them that much when I bought them, then I find I still like them just as much at a later date). And as for fat quarters (pre-cut pieces of fabric, usually 18 x 22in/ 45.5 x 55cm), I cannot get to grips with the supposed usefulness of such small pieces and never buy them because I invariably want or require more.

stash management and storage

Long ago, I took the decision not to build a large fabric stash. This is partly because I don't have anywhere to store a big collection, and partly because I could see that it would be all too easy to keep adding to it by buying fabrics that I thought I may possibly like one day but that in fact would simply stay in the pile forever because I just didn't like them enough. It would be a lazy rather than a decisive way of buying fabrics, and I knew I would later regret many such purchases. Also, I don't keep my fabrics sorted by colour, so never feel that I should be topping up a certain shade or colour (my stash is a lovely mish-mash). I tend to buy with projects in mind, so my collection is actually more of a holding place for fabrics with a destiny than an enormous group of those that are a 'maybe' or 'one day', whose fate has yet to be decided.

Some quilters, however, have wonderful, enormous stashes which they manage and use cleverly. But don't be deceived into thinking that a huge stash automatically produces lovely quilts. It's the way that you use your stash that counts.

As for storage, it pays to look after your fabrics. Keep them flat and neatly folded, out of direct sunlight, and away from heat and odours and anything that might taint or stain them. When I am planning a quilt, I often keep a few piles of fabrics on the floor of my study so that I keep seeing them and thinking about them. Some days I spread them out or rearrange the piles to see how the different combinations work, and I have found that a few weeks out in the open does not harm them as long as they are not left in direct sunlight.

Choosing the quilt design

Once you have fabrics and/ or an idea for a quilt, you are faced with deciding what sort of quilt design to use to express the inspiration and ideas and to make the most of the fabrics. In some cases the design will be obvious; for example, if you have been inspired by the stripes on a deckchair or hammock, you will be planning a quilt made of vertical columns and strips (see Hammock quilt, page 110).

But if you have a pile of beautiful fabrics and aren't sure what to do with them, look at as many books, photos and quilts as you can. Go to the library (see pages 152–53), browse websites and blogs (see page 156), and see what appeals and is within the realm of possibility. Alternatively, play with the fabrics (see page 17) and see what they suggest to you. Maybe you have amassed a collection that features florals, so you could use them in something like the Floral Frocks, Hammock, Tulip Field or Russian Shawl quilts. Or maybe you like small patterns that would look good in a quilt such as the Charming Chintz, Purple Rain or Postage Stamp quilts.

I have learned the hard way to keep my ideas as simple as possible. Much as I adore hand-stitched quilts made up of tiny hexagons and wedding ring quilts with curves and clever intersections, I know that I would never actually finish one; even after making lots of quilts, I have not exhausted all the possibilities of ultra-simple squares, rectangles and strips. It's important not to lose sight of the fact that patchwork is ultimately a matter of cutting fabric and sewing it together; it can be too easy to fall into the trap of thinking that complicated designs must be better because they are harder to make. It's not so. Even if you only ever use squares, you can still make incredible quilts.

So the decision about the design depends on the level of your skills, the amount of time you have and what you want to achieve.

deciding which fabrics to include

I play and sort, and sort and play, for a long time before I cut a single fabric. I make piles, spread out pieces on the floor, and recently I have discovered that unfolding and letting fabrics drop on the floor of a room with good light is amazingly revealing, when they are all seen together in a random placing.

To make fabric decisions easier, I am very clear about the colour scheme I am using. It may be a one- or two-colour theme, but I also have a good idea of the type of colours to use, and this makes it easier to decide which colours to include and which to reject. I take out colours that have the wrong tone or hue and anything that jars or stands out for the wrong reason.

cutting the fabric

Begin by cutting out just a few pieces and building up the layout on the floor or design board (see page 145), and see how it is working. If you cut out everything you have (I have often done this), you may feel that you have accomplished something, but you may also find that you don't use it all because the internal dynamics of the quilt will soon tell you what is working and what isn't. If, however, you are making a two-fabric quilt, you can cut out the whole lot in one go.

arranging and playing

Although I know it can be done, I simply cannot conceive of making decisions about what goes where in a quilt without laying out the whole thing on the floor or design board before making the first stitch. Some quilters can hold a quilt design in their head and create blocks (the units that

make up a quilt) that work perfectly together. Others are happy to use the time-saving shortcut of strip piecing (strips of fabric sewn together before being cut into shapes) and have the ability to successfully predict what will end up where. But I have to see the whole thing before making final placing decisions, and I recommend this strategy to anyone who is new to making quilts. (The only exception is when I am making Log Cabin or Half Log Cabin blocks – see the Purple Rain and Russian Shawl quilts.)

I start by laying out a small part of the quilt. If I am unsure about the way a design will work with the fabrics, I sometimes cut just a few pieces and make a small sample section. So if I am using squares but cannot make up my mind what size they should be, I cut out a few (largest first so that they can be cut down) and use these to decide. Once I am happy with the general design concept, I cut out more pieces and then cut as I go along to save on waste. I then lay out the whole thing on the floor (see page 144 for how to deal with lack of space) until every piece is in its place.

taking risks – what does and doesn't work

Every quilt has a top and a bottom, a right and a wrong way up, so I look at a layout from all angles, often from above (using stepladder, stairs, chair, bed or furniture), or use a reverse magnifying glass – which shows up clearly what isn't working. I leave the layout overnight if possible, because it really helps to see a potential quilt after a period of time before starting to

sew it up. Ask other people to squint at it too. Change pieces or blocks if you are not happy. And if it is truly a disaster, start again: it's much better to do it now than find later that you can't bear to look at the finished quilt.

Be ruthless and weed out colours or patterns that aren't working. Again, it pays to do it at this stage rather than ending up with squares, strips or patches of colour or pattern that annoy you every time you see the finished quilt. Remember that you will be using the quilt for a long time and although the idea of rejecting and throwing out a couple of fabrics may seem a waste of money, it is worth it in the long run.

And how do I know when a fabric isn't working? It jars, or it leaps out of the quilt, or it keeps drawing the eye for a negative reason – perhaps colour, shade, tone, pattern or simply for being the wrong fabric in the wrong place. It's easy to be too timid at this point; far better to take a risk sometimes and add something that you are unsure about but that may work – often you'll be pleasantly surprised at the effect it creates.

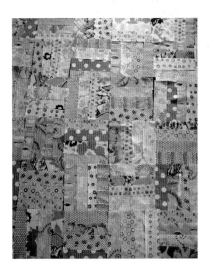

knowing when to stop

If you are making a specific size of quilt, the decision about where to stop doesn't apply. Otherwise, there are a few factors that can help you decide when enough is enough:

The amount of fabric you have:

If you run out of fabric, you may simply have to stop even though you may fall short of the envisaged quilt. But if the alternative is having to spend more time and money buying extra fabrics, would it really make it better? My Hydrangea quilt was supposed to have thirteen lines down, but I ran out of some of the crucial fabrics after twelve lines and simply didn't want the laid-out quilt on the floor for weeks while I waited for half a yard of one fabric to arrive from the US so that I could finish it. This meant having the triangles at the top and bottom of the right-hand side, but that was easy enough to work out. Now the only person who knows that the quilt isn't as planned is ME. No one else has even spotted the error. I love this quilt and I also like the fact that I stopped myself spending money unnecessarily.

When you know that it's looking good, even though it's not as big as you had planned:

The Lisbon Tile and Tulip Field quilts are very different sizes, but with each quilt I stopped when it had reached its optimum size.

When you are seriously out of fabric, time or energy, can't face any more cutting out and sewing together, and want to move on to the next stage:

For example, the Postage Stamp quilt took a long time to cut out and sew up, and when I found I could go no further, I gave in gracefully, which is why it is not an enormous quilt. Remember that quilting is meant to be fun and enjoyable, not a penance.

borders

Most of my early quilts did not have borders. I didn't think borders were necessary and I simply took the quilt right up to the edges. I still like this effect a great deal because it gives density and an old-fashioned feel (lots of vintage quilts don't have borders, probably because there were not enough large pieces of fabric available).

The question of whether or not to add a border (or sashing) is a very personal one. A border is invaluable for making a quilt bigger or framing the design beautifully. (I enjoyed sewing the blocks for the Purple Rain quilt, page 102, but found them time-consuming to make, so I enlarged it by adding a double border – rather than carrying on with the blocks and potentially losing interest.) A border can also be integral to the design, as with the

Swimming Pool quilt, page 124, which has a border to stop people falling into the 'water' and to replicate the tiles around a real pool, and with the Green, Green Grass of Home quilt, page 64, which has a border to suggest a hedge or flower border around a lawn.

The design of the quilt will tell you how wide a border should be. Lay fabrics next to it in different widths and see how they work; a border should not be so wide that it swamps the quilt, and not so thin that it is superfluous. A double border can be very useful for framing a quilt, just as a mount and frame enhances a photo or painting.

Or perhaps you don't want or need a border? Look at the Floral Frocks, Suits and Ties and Postage Stamp quilts (see pages 88, 40 and 94). They simply didn't need any more adding to the design, so I left them alone.

backing fabric

I am always amazed that so often we never see the backs of quilts in books: one of the best aspects of the Kaffe Fassett quilt exhibition in Stockholm in 2006 was the way that some of the quilts were displayed hanging in mid-air, so that both sides were on show. Yet we see both sides of a quilt when we use it – when it gets folded and wrapped, shaken out and thrown about – and I think that choosing the backing fabric is one of the highlights of making a quilt. I have got very excited about the possibilities ever since Susie Green (www.duxhurstquilting.com) introduced me to her way of thinking: that the back should be something of a surprise. The back of a quilt is a wonderful opportunity to choose something unusual and gorgeous. A

back can be simple (dots on Green, Green Grass), complementary (Russian Shawl), meaningful (stripes on Tulip Field to represent the rows of tulips in Holland, or the little 'perforation' dots on Postage Stamp), or extravagant (enormous floral design on Ball Gown), or unexpected (the chandelier print on Beach Huts in the Ice-Cream version).

I generally don't buy backing fabric until I have finished a quilt top. Sometimes I may get backing fabric in advance because it was good value – and even then it must work well (see Floral Frocks, page 88); at other times I have a fabric that must be used because I love it (Purple Rain). I tend to buy the backing fabric from a shop – not from a website – for various reasons: I can fold up the quilt top and take it with me, then play with various combinations in the shop; and I don't have to wait for weeks for fabric to be delivered, or have the disappointment of finding a store has only a tiny quantity left. At the same time, I can buy the wadding because I now know how large the quilt is, choose the quilting thread, and buy the binding

fabric if I don't have enough of a suitable fabric at home.

Two tips: Polka dots always look good on the back of a quilt, and so do large-scale patterns that you love and want to see in their full glory.

wadding

For me, the decision about wadding is never a problem: I use the same one all the time because it is 100 per cent organic cotton, feels as soft as a baby's bottom and has 'scrim', which allows you to keep the stitching lines relatively far apart (up to 8in/ 20cm). It is exactly what Goldilocks would choose, as it is neither too thin nor too thick, but just right. I use Hobbs's Heirloom Organic Cotton with scrim in queen size or king size (it is only available in these two sizes). The offcuts are useful for wrapping fragile things when sending them through the post, and sometimes I find the offcuts include two long lengths which, put together, are enough to go in a smaller quilt (e.g. Suits and Ties, Lisbon Tile quilts). I simply overlap them slightly and make sure I pin the overlap when making the quilt sandwich – quilt top, wadding and backing (no sewing needed, although I am reliably informed that the correct method is to join the two pieces with large crossover stitches such as mattress stitch).

Check the fabric content of wadding before buying it; some are 80 per cent cotton and 20 per cent polyester, and have different recommended maximum distances between quilting lines. Also consider the type of drape you want – the way the quilt folds and hangs. I am not keen on stiff (almost stuffed) quilts, nor on very thin quilts

(unless they are truly vintage). I am fussy about using 100 per cent cotton wadding as the rest of the quilt is 100 per cent cotton (right down to the sewing threads used), and I do not want to compromise with the wadding.

Of course, you don't have to use wadding. You could use a layer of sheeting, an old blanket (I like the idea of using blanket wadding in a woollen quilt that is tied), or a piece of suiting bought cheaply as an end of line (see Suits and Ties quilt, page 40). You can also buy wool or silk or bamboo wadding from quilt shops and websites.

There is no need to pre-wash wadding (some cotton wadding may shrink a little the first time the quilt is washed, but this doesn't bother me). However, do check on the packaging to see what the manufacturer recommends and decide what suits you best. Some people iron or hang up wadding before use to get rid of wrinkles and creases, but I just flatten it as I go along, even though every time I do so I know I should have done it beforehand, as it makes the preparation of the quilt sandwich much easier.

quilting: by hand or machine?

I never have to make a decision here: I always hand-quilt because that's the way I like it. I love all those little stitches running through and up and down my quilt, and I love putting them there. If you are in two minds, here are some things that might help you decide:

- Machine quilting is very quick to do.

- Lines of machine quilting close together give a ridged, flattened effect.

- Hand quilting does not flatten a quilt – in fact, it can often give it more bounce.

- To hand-quilt in a contrasting colour, in the stitch size of your choice, can create additional interest in a quilt.

- Machine quilting creates what looks like an unbroken line, not individual stitches.

- It takes time to quilt by hand, but less time than you think if you just use simple lines spaced quite far apart.

- It can be awkward to quilt on a home sewing machine, and you need a special presser foot.

- You can't watch a brilliant film when machine-quilting, but you can listen to the radio.

- Machine quilting looks great when done on a professional, computerized long-arm quilting machine, using one of the thousands of quilting patterns

available. You may want to find someone to do the quilting for you (e.g. Duxhurst Quilting: www.duxhurstquilting.co.uk).

- You can, of course, hand-quilt with complex patterns and tiny stitches, but it does take time and great skill to trace on the pattern and execute it.

not quilting at all

You may decide that in fact you are not going to quilt at all but instead use a different method of holding the three layers of the quilt sandwich together. Here are some suggestions:

Tying

A very traditional and effective way of securing the layers together, especially if the layers make a thick sandwich that is too thick to go through a machine and too hard on the hands to hand-quilt. Tie at regular intervals such as the intersections or centre of each square. Use wool, embroidery thread or embroidery ribbon in contrasting colours to make the most of the lovely effect. You can find instructions on the Internet.

Buttons

If you have lots of buttons and enjoy sewing them on, you could use them to hold the layers together. I did think of using buttons on the Suits and Ties quilt (see page 40), and even got as far as laying them out, but decided that the prospect of sewing on 140 buttons did not appeal. However, if you were making a small quilt or something like

a cushion cover, a few buttons would look brilliant – and it's a great way to use up old buttons.

threads

I recommend using 100 per cent cotton quilting thread (it's thicker and stronger than all-purpose sewing thread); I prefer to avoid polyester threads as they can age faster than the fabrics they are holding together. I like Mettler quilting thread, because it is ultra-smooth and has a lovely feel when I draw it through the quilt sandwich. Alternatively, use three strands of embroidery cotton (see Ball Gown quilt, page 82), or match the thread to the quilt – use silk threads with silk quilts and tapestry wool for woollen quilts. Choose a colour that either blends or contrasts with the quilt top, depending on your preferences and ideas for the quilt.

quilting pattern (if using)

Decide what sort of quilting pattern you want to create. If you are doing simple quilting by hand, you need to decide where you want the lines to go. I often use diagonals on squares to create interest, and sometimes I work along existing lines to help lead the eye up and down and across the quilt top (please see individual quilt stories for details of how I have quilted each quilt). With every quilt, I aim to create some sort of additional visual interest or harmony with the lines of stitching.

The same applies to quilting by machine, although if you have a sophisticated machine you may be able to program it to create more complex quilting patterns. And if you decide to have the quilting done professionally, you can choose from a huge number of quilting designs.

marking the lines

There are various ways of marking the fabric to indicate quilting lines and patterns. I tried special quilting pencils but couldn't see the lines, and didn't want to use the type of marking pen that requires you to wash it off after quilting to remove the marks. So I improvised with Sellotape or brown parcel tape, which was great for marking lines but a little harsh on the stitches and fabrics when I came to pull it off. Then I started to use masking tape, which was less aggressive, and I haven't looked back. I use long strips to show where to stitch and pull it off gently when I have completed a line. (Used masking tape is also useful for picking up little bits of loose threads and lint as you go along.)

choosing binding fabric

So now you have the three layers of the quilt sandwich joined together by quilting (and have trimmed the edges). It's time to choose a binding fabric.

I select a binding according to the quilt. Sometimes I choose something that is a complete contrast and acts as an outline or narrow frame (Floral Frocks, Postage Stamp). At other times I use something that works with the quilt design and pattern (such as the Russian Shawl quilt, where the binding is part of the sequence of fabrics), or something that does not act as a frame but allows the quilt to extend to the outside edges like a photo that is bled off the edges of a page in a book. (I like

'full-bleed' binding on a colour-themed quilt such as Swimming Pool, Purple Rain, Hydrangea and Amaryllis, where the quilt is an exercise in a strict colour palette, not an exercise in contrasts.)

You may decide to buy a specific fabric or to rummage through your collection. I favour the latter whenever possible, and it is amazing how many fabrics that have been rejected from quilt tops have found their way into bindings – a discarded fabric can come into its own as a binding (and bear in mind that you are only going to see about ½in/ 1cm of it anyway).
Note: Be careful about using fabrics with large dots on bindings, because if the fabric is not cut absolutely straight, the dots will appear wonky.

use

Decide to use and enjoy your quilts. You will not regret it.

tulip
field

This quilt was inspired by an unforgettable end-of-April visit to the tulip fields of Holland. Tulips have been my favourite flower for as long as I can remember, and even though I have seen and grown plenty over the years, nothing quite prepared me for the shock of seeing so many tulips in one place; so many that I wanted to leap into the fields and swoon with joy, totally overcome like Dorothy in the poppy fields in *The Wonderful Wizard of Oz*. It's quite something when you first encounter this flat landscape streaked with long, thin lines of pure colour, and see the way in which the growers transform the view for just a brief moment in the year; the glorious stripes and blocks of densely planted bulbs are breathtaking. The wonderful rectangles and patches of colour looked like a huge paintbox or a vast quilt, and I couldn't *not* make a tulip quilt after such an experience.

Tulips come in all sorts of colours, from the very pale and delicate to the richly deep and definite, and I saw a huge number of colours growing next to each other in the regimented fields in Holland.

However, for this quilt I decided I would restrict the palette to the shades of my very favourite tulips, the ones I grow in the garden, the ones that inspire me every spring. So there are the vivid pinks and magentas of 'China Pink', 'Burgundy' and 'Jacqueline', touches of the deep maroons and purple-blacks of 'Jan Reus', 'Queen of the Night' and 'Café Noir', the bright oranges, tangerines and peaches of 'Apricot Impression', 'Orange Princess', 'Daydream' and 'Dordogne', the lilacs and violets of 'Lilac Wonder', 'Blue Parrot', 'Lilac Perfection', and the paler pinks of 'Menton' and 'Douglas Bader'.

The result is a quilt that captures the richness and vividness of my favourite graceful and elegant tulips in a predominantly warm pink/ orange/ red/ pomegranate colour spectrum and makes me look forward to tulip time all year round.

design

As I wandered around planning my quilt, I realized that I already had the blueprint of a strippy quilt in my Allotment quilt (as seen in *The Gentle Art of Domesticity* and Kaffe Fassett's *Country Garden Quilts*), so all I had to do on my return was to find the right fabrics and grow a textile tulip field.

My Allotment quilt design is simplicity itself and, because of the way it is made, no two quilts will ever be the same, so it offers great scope for new variations on the theme. It uses strips cut from whole widths of fabric and the strips can be any depth you like. All the strips are cut in either full inches or half-inches (no quarters or eighths of an inch), with nothing narrower than 1½in (4cm) (finished measurement, so cut as 2in/ 5cm) and a maximum width of 7in (18cm) or 8in (20cm) (finished measurement). The strips are cut randomly but it's worth cutting specific sections of large-scale fabrics to get the best parts of a pattern, and much of the fun of making this design is discovering how well large patterns cut up in all sorts of widths. Smaller-scale patterns should be used as narrow-strip 'fillers' and 'mixers', because

they tend to deaden the movement of the quilt if used in wide strips. The impact of the quilt is created by the way the big, flamboyant swirls and flowers work with smaller-detail fabrics and together make the eye stop to identify different designs as it roams over the surface.

I added a border because the tulip fields in Holland have borders in the shape of roads, canals or buildings, and I wanted my rows of flowers to be enclosed and to be framed like a large botanical painting.

fabrics

It did occur to me that I should try to include some fabrics with tulips in this quilt, but the truth is that there are very few tulip fabrics that I like. (As if to prove me wrong, Rowan have since produced several wonderful tulip designs by Philip Jacobs.) So in fact there is only one fabric in the top that features tulips, and that is 'Big Blooms' by Kaffe Fassett; it features what look like the rare 'broken' or 'Rembrandt' tulips, and I fussy-cut several rows so that I could get them into the quilt.

As mentioned above, the quilt has a relatively narrow palette – mainly pinks, yellows, oranges and reds, but I enjoyed setting these off with splashes of lime green, sky blue and bronze, all of which reflect the source of the inspiration. I could perhaps have created bolder contrasts, but I was happy with the colourful impact and the fact that I was using up the fabrics I had. I also wanted to experiment with the idea of colours running into each other. Even though the colours stand out and the stripes are vividly demarcated in Holland, I decided to make them flow from row to row in my quilt, so that the lines merge into gorgeous stripes and impressions of colour. The trick is to get each fabric to work with its neighbour to create continuity, richness and depth.

I used fourteen fabrics in the strips. This quilt is a good way to use up any leftover full-width strips; the 'randomness' of the design means that one or two strips of a fabric can be included even though they may not be repeated. On the other hand, it is also just the quilt for showing off some beloved designs to their best advantage in generously wide strips. In my quilt these are the ultra-fabulous 'Big Blooms', the whirling, deep pink Rose 'Stencil Carnation' and the massive 'Lake Blossoms', all by Kaffe Fassett.

Other fabrics include two versions of 'Arbour' from the Lille collection (sadly discontinued), 'Persimmon' (Red), 'Big Blooms' (Red), Arts and Crafts 'Dancing Leaves' (Gold), 'Stencil Carnation' (Rose), 'Lake Blossoms' (Red), 'Bekah' (Orange) and 'Cabbage Patch' (Magenta), all by Kaffe Fassett, plus 'Coneflower' and 'Mum Toss' (Orange) by Martha Negley, and 'Lilac Rose' (Lilac) and 'Grandiose' (Ochre) by Philip Jacobs. The border and part of the backing is 'Silhouette Rose' (Wine) by Kaffe Fassett, and this also appears in some strips.

On the back I used 'Ava Rose' by Tanya Whelan for Freespirit. This is a very fresh, modern version of the classic ticking stripe in fuchsia pink and white, which echoes the idea of stripes and rows of tulips while at the same time providing the perfect contrast to the densely patterned quilt top. To keep down the cost of the quilt backing, I bought only two widths of the fabric and added a strip of the border fabric to extend the back to the necessary width.

The binding is a bright and cheerful yellow fabric that picks out one of the theme colours. This is from the Linden fabric collection by Melissa Saylor for P&B Textiles.

✎ materials

Fabric suggestions: This quilt works well in a defined palette with contrasting highlights (as here), or in a broader palette that contains more colours (but they do need to be of similar depths and tones).

- - - - - - - - - - - - - - - - - - - -

Quilt top: It is a large quilt, which will fit on a king-sized bed. To make the quilt top (excluding border), you will need a total of approximately 5–5½yd/ m in a mixture of *full-width* ½yd/ m and ¼yd/ m pieces, although any full-width pieces from 2in (5cm) upwards can be used. If you have more or less fabric, you can make the quilt longer or shorter. You may want to have two or three 'lead' fabrics, in which case you will need ¾yd/ m of each.

To make a 5in (12.5cm) border, you will need 44in (112cm) of fabric. Notes: You could buy a metre or yard of fabric and reduce the border to 4in (10cm) (finished width); a border is not essential – see below.

- - - - - - - - - - - - - - - - - - - -

The quilt has random-width strips in two columns, with a border.

Backing: To make the backing for a quilt this size, you will need to allow for a third width of fabric, which can become expensive. My way of overcoming this is to use two full widths and extend the backing to the necessary width by adding an extra strip along one side. This strip can be of a second or leftover fabric. Alternatively, if you omit the border, two widths of fabric will be enough to back the quilt top.

To make a two-width backing, you will need 5½yd (5m) of fabric, plus a strip of fabric(s) measuring 13 x 97in (33 x 246cm) to extend the width. If you prefer to have a backing made of a single fabric, you will need 8yd (7.3m) of fabric.

- - - - - - - - - - - - - - - - - - - -

Binding: You will need 25in (64cm) fabric to make the binding.

- - - - - - - - - - - - - - - - - - - -

You will also need:

➤ A king-sized piece of wadding 3–4in (7.5–10cm) larger all around than the quilt top (I use 100 per cent organic cotton with scrim).
➤ 100 per cent cotton all-purpose sewing thread in ecru or taupe for the machine piecing.
➤ 100 per cent cotton quilting thread.

- - - - - - - - - - - - - - - - - - - -

Final measurements: 86½ x 89in (220 x 226cm) or the size of a decent tulip bed.

✎ directions

All seam allowances are ¹⁄₄in (6mm) unless otherwise stated.

— The quilt top is made with strips cut from the full width of the fabric, and the strips are pieced into two columns, which are joined to form the centre of the quilt. There is no set pattern to the strips, which are cut in random lengths and laid out according to taste.

— Cut out the strips from selvedge to selvedge. Vary the widths from 2–8in (5–20cm), cutting everything to the nearest inch or half-inch. It is possible to cut out more than one strip at a time, but I prefer to vary the strip sizes of each fabric, so cut out each strip separately. I also cut out in batches, not all in one go.

— It may come as a surprise that there is a noticeable variation in the widths of quilting fabrics, even those from the same manufacturer. There are two ways of dealing with this:

(a) Either trim all the strips to the same width (I would suggest 39in/ 99cm);

(b) Or trim the selvedges and sew the strips together, keeping the edge that will be in the centre of the quilt as straight as possible and then trim the entire edge of the column. (So when piecing the left half, you need to keep the inside edge, i.e. right-hand side, as straight and even as possible, and when piecing the right half you need to keep the inside, i.e. left-hand edge, as straight as possible. No matter what you do, you will have to trim to the lowest common denominator, i.e. the narrowest fabric.) This is the method I use.

— Once you have cut out some strips, start making the layout. This is a very easy quilt to lay out as changes can be made very quickly, and new fabrics added if desired. Cut out more strips as you go along. Scrutinize the quilt regularly from all sides (or use a reverse magnifying glass).

— When you are happy with the design, sew the strips together to make the two main sections, keeping the inside edge as straight and even as possible. When sewing the strips, remember to alternate the direction of sewing, i.e. start each seam at the end of the last, working from right to left, then left to right to prevent the top going out of shape. If you find you forget where you finished the last seam, place a pin at the correct end before you cut the thread.

— Trim the edges. Note than the two sides do not have to be exactly the same width (mine are 37in/ 94cm and 38in/96.5cm) unless you want them to be the same.

— Iron each side, pressing the seams in one direction. Press the seams on one side in one direction, and on the other in the opposite direction.

— Join the two sides at the centre. Iron and press the central seam to one side.

— Cut out 5½in (14cm) full-width strips for the border. Sew together to make longer strips as necessary.

— Sew the border strips to the sides first and trim. Iron, pressing the seams towards the outside edge.

— Now sew the borders to the top and bottom edges. Trim, iron and press. The quilt top is now complete.

— Make the backing by sewing together the widths of fabric with ½in (1cm) seams. The backing should be 3–4in (7.5–10cm) longer and wider all around than the quilt top – in this case 95 x 97in (241 x 246cm). If using two widths, extend the backing with an extra piece of matching/ non-matching fabric measuring approximately 13 x 97in (33 x 246cm). Iron and press the seam(s) open.

— Make the quilt sandwich (see page 142). Trim the quilt edges so that the wadding and backing is about 2in (5cm) larger than the quilt top.

— Hand-quilt with simple running stitches in a matching or contrasting thread (I used a peachy coral). Use the seams as guidelines, sewing ¹⁄₄in (6mm) away from the line, and stitch lines every 4in (10cm) or so, according to where the seams are. You can either stitch up to the edge of the quilt or to the edge of the strips, and then add a line of stitching around the border.

— Trim the quilt top with scissors or rotary cutter.

— Make and attach the binding (see page 143 for further instructions).

— Tiptoe carefully among your tulips.

fabric inspiration

One of the main points of this book is to emphasize the value of using very simple designs and creating impact and effect with fabulous fabrics. Of course, this would not be possible if there were not so many beautiful fabrics available these days in shops and on the Internet.

Yet despite the revolution in recent years in quilt fabric design (if you compare what is available now to what was available, say, twenty years ago, when you would have had to rely greatly on clever, complex designs to create impact and effect, you will see that there has been a revolution), we very rarely read or hear about the fabric design process. As you look at a lovely design, you may wonder what inspires the designers whose fabrics you are using and what kind of creative process lies behind the end product. So, as this book is about inspiration, I thought I would ask a couple of my favourite fabric designers about their sources of inspiration and how they translate into the fabrics we see.

Kaffe Fassett

If you are a knitter or a quilter, a maker of mosaics, a stitcher of needlepoint or a lover of colour, the chances are that you already know of Kaffe Fassett, one of the most inspirational figures in the world of textiles (and more). He came to a grey, overcast England in the 1960s and brought with him all the energy, warmth and colour of his native California, and he has been encouraging us to use all three qualities in our knitting and stitching ever since. Kaffe is a painter and a designer who has written many books, but he is also an indefatigable doer and maker, and is never without a creative project to hand. He has the most incredible eye for colour and pattern, and is not afraid of either. His message is simple: surround yourself with lovely yarns and fabrics, cast aside all inhibitions about taste and aspirations of perfection, and make something that you like.

Kaffe moved into the world of patchwork and quilting in the 1990s when Liza Prior Lucy, the well-known American quilter, urged him to give it a go, as she was convinced his talents were perfectly suited to this particular branch of textiles. She was right, and since then they have written three books together (see inspirational books, pages 152–53) and collaborated on countless more projects and publications, including the annual Rowan *Patchwork and Quilting* books.

Kaffe began designing fabrics for quilting after the publication, in 1997, of his first book – *Patchwork* – when he found that the desire to create quilts in his personal style was restricted by the fabrics that were on offer at that time. I can still remember seeing Kaffe's first designs in 2003 at the American Museum in Bath, when I went to see his 'Quilt Bonanza' exhibition; I had never seen anything like them before. They were filled with vibrant colour in clever and startling combinations and some had huge, exuberant designs that broke the mould of quilt fabric design – much to my delight. I came home with a bag full of fabrics and my quilting suddenly took a whole new direction. Kaffe has that kind of effect.

What motivates him now, above all, is the desire to provide a rich palette for quilters that goes beyond the more restricted colour range offered by most fabric companies. Because of his artistic background, Kaffe tends to use fabrics as a painter uses paints; he couldn't imagine a paintbox without stimulating tones, so why should a quilter be without them?

The inspiration for the designs comes from every corner of the world's decorative arts and cultural patterns. As anyone who has ever listened to Kaffe speak about colour and inspiration will know, he has accumulated and collected the most amazing set of visual references on which to draw. Unsurprisingly, the strongest influences are those places and cultures that have a joyous use of colour and a boldness of design. So Islamic carpets, Scandinavian painted furniture, and Oriental fabrics and porcelain all mix with memories, photos, books and artefacts brought back from Mexico, Africa, India, China and Japan. To add a dash of trademark zest, humour and drama, Kaffe turns to the circus and theatre; these sources of inspiration also explain the sense of scale, showmanship and pure entertainment that Kaffe's quilts exude. He picks up all this inspiration on his travels, in museums, at the theatre and from books.

The planning and production of his fabric collections is quite a feat and there is little time to rest in between; as one fabric collection is launched (look on the website of Westminster Fibers – see www.westminsterfibers.com – to find out what is coming next), Kaffe starts to assemble a list of possible subjects for the next collection(s). He designs as he knits, with no particular plan, but letting the collection develop organically. So he may say, vaguely, that he would like to come up with two or three florals, a couple of texture prints, and perhaps a stripe. But in fact – and this is the joy of seeing each new collection when it appears – there will always be some surprises because Kaffe tries to create a collection of fabrics that you or I might have put together from trips to charity shops or flea markets (themed and 'matchy-matchy' collections are not for him). He likes the idea of chance, of surprise and serendipitous finds that work well together without necessarily matching perfectly.

When it comes to making the actual designs, Kaffe draws out the forms in repeat and then paints them in gouache. He photocopies five copies of the original artwork and paints the various colours over them and, apart from using a computer to check repeats and provide copies, everything else is done by hand. (I have seen some of Kaffe's hand-painted designs and they are things of beauty that I would happily frame and hang on my wall.)

And how does Kaffe the colour genius decide which colours to use? As you would expect, he never imposes a rigid set of rules on himself. Rather, he has certain rough rules of thumb. He usually includes a deep blue colourway, a red, and a brown or yellow. Then he likes to try a very soft pastel version for more quiet and feminine quilts. He also tries to visualize the sorts of palettes and variations needed for the creation of successful quilts and puts himself in the position of the quilter (as he later will be, when working in collaboration with Liza Prior Lucy) and asks himself how she/ he would use these fabrics. But how does he make every single colourway so desirable? The answer is that he works by instinct and with no real plan, except to create the sorts of fabrics he himself would enjoy using.

With every collection, Kaffe hopes to inspire quilters with his playful, daring and exuberant use of colour and by the sheer scale of the prints. When he first started designing fabrics, there was a marked resistance in the quilting world to the large (some might say gloriously huge) scale of his floral designs, which had been inspired by furnishing fabrics (when he first started with quilts he used furnishing fabrics, because he couldn't find quilt-weight designs to match his vision and express his style). But over time Kaffe has won widespread admiration and acclaim by breaking through so-called rules of what is right, possible and in good taste, to establish a new way of thinking about quilts and to inspire a new wave of colour-hungry quilters.

beach
hut

This quilt, which comes in two versions, Candy and Ice-Cream, is inspired by the traditional painted beach huts that can be found on English beaches such as Southwold in Suffolk and Whitstable in Kent. These beach huts are a marvellous source of inspiration for any quilter who likes to walk along beaches, do some beachcombing and dream of owning a little hut in which to shelter from the British weather, make a cup of tea, sit under a blanket (or quilt) and keep warm while watching the waves.

What I particularly like about beach huts is their home-made look, the fact that the best ones are personalized, painted in jaunty colours and clearly loved by their owners. I also admire the way that their lines, being hand-painted and then weather-beaten, are not always perfect, and I enjoy the way they present a relaxed, uncoordinated character. All in all, they are ideal inspiration for quilters who care more about colour and character than perfect execution. I was also influenced by the way in which the Gee's Bend quilters take similar inspiration from the architecture and buildings that surround them, no matter how ordinary, ramshackle and run-down (*Gee's Bend: The Architecture of the Quilt*, ed. Paul Arnett et al., Tinwood Books).

As for colours, both quilts take further inspiration from the seaside. The Candy version contains colours we find in all the major British seaside resorts in summer: stalls full of teeth-rotting cerise rock and candy pink sugar shrimps, occasional sightings of bright blue skies with scudding white clouds, the deep aquas of the North Sea on a good day, bright annual flowers in municipal beds and gardens, and the orange of the sun and sand. The Ice-Cream version is deliberately paler and inspired by ice-creams sold in old-fashioned ice-cream parlours such as the fabulously unchanged Morelli's in Broadstairs, with its peach-coloured glass, cream mock leather banquette and wonderful pastel-coloured ice-cream sundaes.

design

I have been making detours to look at beach huts for years and have long wanted to make a simple quilted version, but was put off by the idea of needing a roof on each hut (and thus getting into the business of triangles). But after a more recent walk on Whitstable beach, when I looked at and photographed the various stripes of the beach huts, I realized that it was these stripes that I wanted to use most of all. So I simplified and simplified the source of inspiration until I came to the four-stripe square blocks that are placed in an alternating horizontal and vertical pattern in the way that the directions of the beach hut stripes vary from hut to hut.

I sketched and worked out what size of strip to use and settled on 2 x 8in (5 x 20cm) (finished size), although the beauty of this design is that it can be done on any scale as long as the four strips make a square i.e. the combined short ends equal the long side, so you could use 1 x 4in (2.5 x 10cm), 3 x 12in (7.5 x 30cm), 4 x 16in (10 x 40.5cm) and so on. I chose 2 x 8in (5 x 20cm) because I wanted to show off a few small fabric patterns, which might otherwise have got lost in larger strips. This quilt design also offered a chance to discover how brilliantly and surprisingly well many bigger patterns cut up.

I didn't have enough fabric to make a huge quilt, so settled on seven blocks across and nine blocks down, but I would emphasize that this is a quilt that can very easily be made smaller or larger – just keep adding the blocks. I made mine into a size to fit a single bed – or perhaps a one-person quilt for keeping warm in a beach hut or on a breezy day at the beach, or while eating a huge knickerbocker glory.

The basic design offered so many possibilities to play with lovely fabrics and interesting colours that I decided to make two versions. In fact, I could go on using it over and over again, and still enjoy building up squares from four strips.

fabrics

Candy version

I soon discovered that this is a great design for playing with colour. It could be made in just two colours, the way many beach huts are painted (e.g. red and white), or you could restrict each square to two colours, but I decided to use some pink, blue and aqua fabrics that had been gravitating towards the same 'holding pile' (see page 16) for a while without a clear purpose. These make for a bright, sun-washed quilt with a few splashes of deeper yellows and deep marine blues.

Once I'd decided on the beach theme, it was easy to select fabrics. There's an amazing Joelle Hoverson 'Cake Rock Beach' fabric in a stone/ blood-red colourway (that shouldn't work but does), with its beautifully drawn corals and seaweed that I fussy-cut in order to get the motifs on the strips. The Kobayashi 'Chrysanthemums', a wavy, sea-like Japanese fabric might have been too pastel but fits in well, and the Jennifer Paganelli/ Sis Boom white-on-sky-blue and candy-pink-on-white 'Casey Scroll' designs work as unifying fabrics. Walking over this quilt is like beachcombing, picking out the flotsam and jetsam of the big designs that have been cut up and taken apart and can be found floating in the quilt.

Right: Candy version

Other fabrics include Kaffe Fassett's 'Big Blooms' in Duck Egg and 'Stencil' in Scarlet, a pretty Yuwa 'Crazy Daisy', a few strips of a prized vintage feedsack fabric, Philip Jacobs's 'Garden Leaves', 'Garden Party' and 'Tropical', all in Celadon, and two floral fabrics featuring anemones and chrysanthemums from the Covent Garden collection by Fabric Freedom for Benartex. I used fourteen fabrics, some in tiny quantities and others more extensively.

Choosing a backing fabric was great fun; it had to be something fresh and breezy but not pink (too much sugar can ruin your teeth and quilts), and when I found 'Chrysanthemum' in Amy Butler's Belle collection in a piercing forget-me-not blue, I was thrilled. Then I chose a coral pink and deep turquoise 'Petals' fabric by Tina Givens for Freespirit as a contrastingly dark, but not too dark, frame that intensified the colours of the quilt.

Ice-Cream version

I liked the outcome of the Candy quilt so much, and had a pile of sandy and watery fabrics that I didn't know what to do with, that I decided to see if they would work in this design. I thought that maybe the fabrics might look washed out and bland. But I went through them all over again and saw that they could cope with the addition of a few stronger colours and, indeed, they began to look far more interesting.

This quilt took 'peaches and cream' as a first guiding principle and then branched out into ice-cream/ sandy beach/ dots of blue sky/ pale sea colours, until I had a very 'English beach in summer' or ' ice-cream parlour' effect. The majority of the fabrics lack real intensity of colour – they are all very pretty versions of colours – but they are of the same tonal value. I used seventeen in total, and rejected a few that were too deep, including a very intense orange that I thought contained

the right colours but which turned out to be of the wrong tone.

The fabrics include a medley of Kaffe Fassett designs (he does pastels brilliantly): a lime and lilac 'Pansy', 'Stencil' in Gold and Lilac, 'Asha' in Grey, an out-of-print 'Auricula', and 'Russian Rose' in Pastel. Then there is a 'Flea Market Fancy' design by Denyse Schmidt, a lovely 'Tea Cups' design in Aqua by Martha Negley, and two Freshcut 'Graphic Mum' prints by Heather Bailey. There are also a number of Japanese fabrics that I bought in very small quantities from Purl Patchwork (www.purlsoho.com) because they were expensive – but have proved to be worth every penny. These are the 'hand-drawn' dots, the pale, peachy, winding floral and a kimono-style landscape that cuts up into fantastic abstract strips.

Not long after I'd done the layout and was out of the room, a quilting fairy came along and placed strips of the dusty pink and white large spot (fabric I had cut but rejected) strategically throughout the quilt, totally transforming it. This was my daughter Phoebe, revealing herself as an excellent secret quilt consultant.

I went to town when choosing the backing fabric. It would have been too easy to settle for a matching but unsurprising dot or small-scale design, and when I found the wild and whimsical Fairy Tip-Toes 'Chandelier Medallion' by Tina Givens for Freespirit, I knew I'd found the right fabric. It matches my ideas of how I imagine a posh ice-cream parlour – or even a posh beach hut – would look with wacky chandeliers.

The binding is simple. It's a peachy dot, 'Spring Fling' by Me and My Sister Designs for Moda; it frames the quilt and picks out the colour of the bird cameo on the back.

Right: Ice-Cream version

ave we trials and temptations:
  Is there trouble anywhere?
e should never be discouraged:
  Take it to the Lord in prayer!
an we find a Friend so faithful,
  Who will all our sorrows share?
esus knows our every weakness—
  Take it to the Lord in prayer!

e we weak and heavy-laden,
Cumbered with a load of care?
ur, still our Refuge—
  the Lord in prayer!
s despise. forsake thee?
  the Lord in prayer!
 His arms He'll take and shield thee,
Thou wilt find a solace there.

JE   my soul,
While   hy Bosom fly.
  Wh   g waters roll.
Hide   st still is high:
Till   Saviour. hide.
Safe   of life is past:
O   en guide.
             oul at last.

             I none:
             ss soul on Thee:
heave me not alone.
             nd comfort me.
             Thee is stay'd.
                      bring:

                      wing.

                      want:
                      find:
                      faint,
                      the blind.

I am all unrighteousness:
  Vile and full of sin I am.
  Thou art full of Truth

Plenteous grace with
  Grace to cleanse

Dare to have a purpose firm!
  Dare to make it known!

Many mighty men are lost,
  Daring not to stand,
Who for God had been a host,
  By joining Daniel's Band.

Many giants, great and tall,
  Stalking through the land,
Headlong to the earth would fall,
  If met by Daniel's Band.

Hold the gospel banner high!
  On to victory grand!
Satan and his host defy,
  And shout for Daniel's Band!

7.5.7.6.

THERE'S a Friend for little children
  Above the bright blue sky,
A Friend Who never changes,
  Whose love will never die:
Our earthly friends may fail us,
  And change with changing years,
This Friend is always worthy
  Of that dear Name He bears.

There's a home for little children
  Above the bright blue sky,
Where Jesus reigns in glory,
  A home of peace and joy:
No home on earth is like it,
  Nor can with it compare:
For every one is happy,
       be happier, there.

Th   for little children
        ht blue sky,
A   that will not weary,
        sung continually,
A   which even Angels
         never, never sing:
         know not Christ as Saviour,
         worship Him as King.

         a robe for little children
         the bright blue sky:
         harp of sweetest music
         palms of victory,
         above is treasured,
         found in Christ alone:
         rant Thy little children
         ow Thee as th   wn.

Waving wanderers onward
  To their home on high.

Jesu, Lord and Master,
  At Thy sacred feet,
Here with hearts rejoicing
  See Thy children meet:
Often have we left Thee,
  Often gone astray:
Keep us, mighty Saviour,
  In the narrow way.

All our days direct us
  In the way we go,
Lead us on victorious
  Over every foe:
Bid Thine angels shield u
  When the storm-clouds
Pardon Thou and save us
  In the last dread hour

O WORSHIP the King,
  All-glorious above:
O gratefully sing
  His power and His love:
Our Shield and Defender,
  The Ancient of Days,
Pavilioned in Splendour,
  And girded with praise.

O tell of His might,
  O sing of His grace,
Whose robe is the light,
  Whose canopy, space:
His chariots of wrath
  Deep thunder-clouds form,
And dark is His path
  On the wings of the orm

The earth with its store
  Of wonders untold,
Almighty, Thy power
  Hath founded of old,
Hath stablished it fast
  By a changeless decree,
And round it hath cast,
  Like a mantle, the sea.

Thy bountiful care
  What tongue can recite
It breathes in the air,
  It shines in the light,
It streams from the hills,
  It descends to the plai
And sweetly distils
  In the dew and the rain

materials

Fabric suggestions: Gather twelve to twenty fabrics if you want to make a quilt similar to mine in style (I used fourteen in the Candy version and seventeen in the Ice-Cream version), fewer if you have fewer or want to make a less variegated quilt. Play with them, making line-ups and changing the order frequently, as you may discover a fabric looks awful next to one fabric but great surrounded by others. Don't be afraid to try what might appear to be no-go fabrics; it only takes a moment to put a fabric in, take a squint at it, and remove if necessary (I discarded two in the Candy version: a lovely pink print that was simply too pale, and a yellow print that stood out too much because the yellow was too ochre). On the other hand, you might discover a wonderful new combination that sets off the whole quilt. This is what happened when I introduced the pink and white spot and the huge 'Russian Rose' fabrics into the Ice-Cream version.

- - - - - - - - - - - - - - - - -

Quilt top: You will need a mix of ½yd/ m and ¼yd/ m pieces and smaller offcuts or cherished scraps, to make up a minimum of 4½yd/ m. I prefer not to begin with a set yardage; instead I simply gather what I have and do not worry about the possibility of leftovers. So I would always start with more than 4½yd/ m and then use what is needed. Ten to twelve fabrics will be enough to give a good variety and a few more could enhance the mix.

Back of Candy   Back of Ice-Cream

Backing: You will also need 4½yd/ m of fabric for the backing (this gives enough allowance for a large-scale repeat like the ones I have used).

- - - - - - - - - - - - - - - - -

Binding: The binding for a quilt this size takes 17½in (44.5cm) of fabric.

- - - - - - - - - - - - - - - - -

You will also need:

- A piece of wadding 3–4in (7.5–10cm) larger all around than the quilt top (I use 100 per cent organic cotton with scrim).
- 100 per cent cotton all-purpose sewing thread in ecru or taupe for the machine piecing.
- 100 per cent cotton quilting thread.

- - - - - - - - - - - - - - - - -

Finished measurements: 56½ x 72½in (143.5 x 184cm).

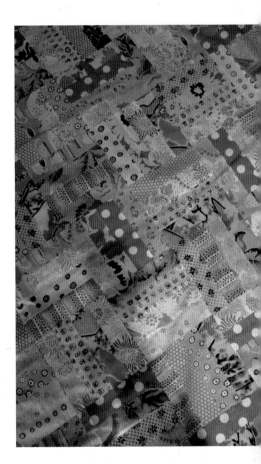

Ice-Cream

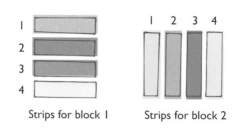

Strips for block 1   Strips for block 2

Top section of quilt
The quilt has seven blocks across and nine blocks down.

✎ directions

All seam allowances are ¼in (6mm) unless otherwise specified.

— Don't start by cutting out all your fabric at once. Instead, cut out a few strips from each of the possible fabrics and play with them. Once you know what does and does not work, cut out more. I cut out in three or four batches for each quilt, to avoid wastage of fabrics that did not turn out as well as expected.

— All strips need to be cut to 2½ x 8½in (6 x 21.5cm) to make finished strips 2 x 8in (5 x 20cm), which then make each finished square 8 x 8in (20 x 20cm). Cut out up to four

strips at a time by folding the fabric in half selvedge to selvedge, then in half again, and then cutting with the rotary cutter and ruler.

— It would be less time-consuming to strip-piece the blocks, i.e. sew together four long strips of fabric, cut into 8½in (21.5cm) blocks and place in different parts of the quilt. But I do not work this way as I don't want repeating blocks, especially if they don't turn out as well as I'd hoped. So I take the longer, more painstaking method and place every single strip separately – and this way I have complete control over what goes where and the overall balance of the quilt. Plus it is really enjoyable just playing with strips of fabric and it doesn't take too long (about a morning, with a few breaks

for tea so that I have a more critical eye when I return).

— Build up the quilt layout until you have the size you want/ like (but remember to adjust the requirements for backing and binding fabrics and wadding if you are making it larger or smaller). Mine is seven squares across and nine squares down.

— Stand back and appraise the quilt. Allow your eye to move over it, looking for problem areas. Do you have too many stand-out fabrics leaping out at you in the wrong places? Can you see fabrics repeated or too close together where you don't want them? Is there another fabric that could be introduced to enliven/ balance the effect?

— Don't forget to change your vantage point so that you are looking critically from different angles.

— Once you are happy with the layout, you need to sew together each block. I do this by picking up the four strips in the correct order, taking them to the machine, sewing them, and returning the newly made square to its correct place in the layout. This is so I don't lose track of what goes where – something that is very easy to do.

— If you don't have the time and space to leave the layout on the floor, you need to make a little pile of strips for each square and number it with a Post-It note pinned through the pile, so that you know where it belongs (e.g. row 2, square 3).

— Once you have machine-pieced all the squares, it's time to iron them. Pick up the squares in columns or rows – I prefer to work in columns with this design (number the top square for each column or row and keep the pile together). Press all seams to one side, keeping the same direction on every square. So I ironed all horizontal stripe squares with the seams facing downwards, and all the vertical stripe squares with the seams facing to the right. Iron all the right sides, too.

— Now sew the squares into strips, creating rows across or columns down and keeping them clearly numbered. Iron each strip, pressing the seams in alternating directions, e.g. odd rows facing up and even rows facing down, or vice versa.

— Machine-piece the top with the strips of squares by sewing them together in the right order (it's only after this that you can discard the Post-It notes and pin numbering system, although I always leave the top left marker in until the binding has been attached). Iron again, this time pressing all the new seams in the same direction.

— Make the backing by sewing together two widths of fabric with a ½in (1cm) seam, making sure that the back is 3–4in (7.5–10cm) larger all round than the quilt top. (You can trim the selvedges of the backing fabric if you like, but I don't bother.) Press the seam open.

— Make the quilt sandwich and pin (see page 142 for more information on making the sandwich).

— Hand-quilt with 100 per cent cotton quilting thread. I used a pale, dusty pink thread on the Ice-Cream quilt and sky blue on the Candy quilt to make a grid of running stitches. Follow horizontal and/ or vertical seams and stitch lines ¼in (6mm) away from the seam. Alternatively, machine-quilt if you prefer.

— Take the quilt to the beach with a flask of tea, a warm jumper and a good book. Or, if it's warm, sit on it while you eat seaside rock and ice-cream in the sun.

More architectural quilt inspiration:

Gee's Bend: The Architecture of the Quilt, ed. Paul Arnett et al. (Tinwood Books).

suits and ties

A few years ago, when clearing out a wardrobe, I found dozens of ties belonging to Simon, my husband. The problem was that he, like so many other increasingly informally attired office workers, was no longer wearing these variously smart, bright, witty and cleverly detailed ties, but I could not bear to see them going to waste. So I took a pile to a weekend workshop with textile artist Janet Bolton (www.janetbolton.com) and made a textile picture with them (centre photo, left), and I called this picture, which turned out remarkably like a mini-quilt, *Ties Must Be Worn*. From then on, the idea of a large-scale quilt using tie silks or a tie theme would not go away, but it wasn't until I chanced upon some lengths of beautiful wool suiting and an amazing selection of uncut tie silks on the same day, but in two different London shops, that I came up with the idea of a literal suits and ties quilt.

Traditional men's wool suits and silk ties are made with the most beautiful, high-quality fabrics and I was keen to work with a few before they are consigned to oblivion and disappear from the shelves of tailors' suppliers and specialist fabric shops. So I could not resist buying two end-of-line lengths of suiting – one tweedy and one made from wool and cashmere with 'Made in England' woven proudly along the selvedge – for a bargain price from a shop in Berwick Street in London. I fell in love with the feel of the fabrics and their wonderful muted colours, and initially thought of using them with some of Simon's old striped cotton work shirts – but then I wandered further down Berwick Street to The Cloth House and found a treasure trove of silk tie fabrics on bolts. It was amazing to see these fabrics as a piece rather than in a tie and to be able to appreciate fully the beauty of the weave, the cleverness of the jacquard technique, the wonderful thickness of the silk, the sheen and the deep, rich colours.

The mix of woollen fabrics and gorgeous colours led me to another source of inspiration: the traditional woollen hearth quilts made by English and Welsh quilters using scraps and pieces of old wool fabrics from clothes and blankets, hand-stitched or tied with wool. These two strands of inspiration make this quilt a mix of Savile Row elegance and good, old-fashioned thrift.

design

Fine woollen and silk fabrics can be tricky to cut on a mat with a rotary cutter and ruler, as they tend to slip out of place even under the pressure of the ruler (you need to take care that all the edges are aligned at all times). Also, thick silk frays all too easily and its delicate fibres can stick to dry hands. With these difficulties in mind, I decided it would be best to keep to a design of very simple squares and to handle them as little as possible.

I did toy with the idea of a clever suits and ties design based on traditional Bow Tie quilts, but rejected this on two counts: first, a straightforward design would show off the fabrics to their best advantage and second, because my wool and silk fabrics are thicker than quilting cottons and would create bulky seams, I did not want to use them in small pieces to make bigger blocks.

So I went for 4in (10cm) squares (finished size) that showcase the fabrics nicely, are easy to handle and build up into a quilt top quickly. Since I had two clearly contrasting piles of fabrics (dark woollens and bright silks), the most obvious and effective design was a chequerboard. I particularly like the contrast of the basic design (something a child would make) and the sophisticated fabrics (that grown-ups would wear).

I decided against a border, as the top looked to me like an old-fashioned quilt you would use to keep your lower half warm when sitting by the fire (or even as a car quilt, for wrapping cold legs on long journeys). The dark colours mean that this is a durable quilt which can withstand a little outdoor or fireside use, so I kept it very plain and simply added a dark binding, made out of the plainer suit fabric.

But I did want the quilting to stand out, and it does in fact make all the difference to the look of the quilt. I had thought that large stitches (like the ones tailors use when tacking made-to-measure suits) would look good and had happily quilted half the quilt top when I realized that no one could tell the stitches were there because they were in charcoal grey. So I undid them all and started again with a deep gold thread, and this time the tacking stood out and made the quilt look completely different.

fabrics

I bought a couple of two-metre lengths of relatively sober plain suiting at the ridiculously cheap price of £5 a piece (the normal cost is around £35 per metre) from Textile King, a specialist tailoring shop on Berwick Street in London. One is a very fine charcoal-grey wool/ cashmere blend suiting with the faintest of red and bottle green stripes, and the other is a heavier houndstooth check in grey and black, but also with dark green and blood red stripes. To these I added squares of dark grey wool with a fine yellow stripe from an old skirt.

For contrast, I used nine different silk tie fabrics, all bought from The Cloth House in London. I had the suiting fabrics with me and chose a range of tie fabrics that worked well together within a general colour theme (rusty orange, gold, navy blue, bright blue and lavender). I could quite easily have chosen all stripes to make a quilt that wouldn't look out of place in a gentlemen's club or boarding school, but instead deliberately chose a mix of stripes plus some less traditional motifs such as bear paws, lobsters and flamingos, all within a colour theme of gold, coral and blue.

For the backing, I knew I wanted to develop the businesswear theme to include shirts, but as I did not have enough of Simon's old shirts to cut up into a patchwork backing, I decided that the next best thing would be to use shirting fabric off the roll. There are some wonderful shirt stripes and checks available from old-fashioned fabric stores, and I was lucky enough to find one that features the main colours of the top (grey, blue and orange). At 72in (183cm) wide, this fabric is a gift to the quilter.

✎ materials

It is difficult to give exact requirements because these suit and garment fabrics come in all sorts of widths; suiting and shirting can be up to 72in (183cm) wide, whereas tie fabric is often only 36in (91.5cm) wide. You may prefer to use recycled fabrics from old garments, scrap bags and charity shops, in which case it is more useful to know how many squares you need. So here are two sets of requirement guidelines:

Starting from scratch quilt:

- Lightweight woollen fabric used to make suits, jackets or skirts: 15in (38cm) (or ½yd/ m) each of three or four, 72in (183cm) wide.
- Woven silk tie fabrics (or any silk fabric): 10in (25cm) each of eight to ten, 36in (91.5cm) wide (approx.).

Backing: 2yd/ m of 72in (183cm) cotton shirting fabric; OR 4yd/ m of 42–45in (106–114cm) quilt fabric (an expensive option, as there will be a great deal of leftover fabric); OR 2yd/ m quilt fabric plus an 18 x 72in (45 x 183cm) strip of another fabric (or several fabrics) to sew to the main fabric to widen the backing.

Thrift quilt:

- Collect an equal number of suits and ties squares. To make a quilt the same size as the one pictured, you will need 104 'tie' squares and 104 'suits' squares. However, your quilt could be any number of squares wide and long and in any size of square (although this will be restricted by the narrowness of the ties you have). If you are short of ties/ silks, you could make a mostly wool quilt with a few silk highlights and brighten it up further with coloured stitching, or use different types of highlight fabrics (e.g. cut from old dresses and jackets).

Backing: Make a patchwork backing 3–4in (7.5–10cm) larger all around than the quilt top, with pieces of fabric cut from recycled shirts.

Binding for either quilt: You will need 10in (25cm) of a 72in (183cm) wool suiting or 15in (38cm) of a 42–45in (106–114cm) cotton quilt fabric.

Finished measurements: 53 x 65in (134.5 x 165cm). See Resources (page 158) for where to buy fabrics.

directions

Notes

- Use a ¼in (6mm) seam allowance throughout unless otherwise indicated.

- Press all seams OPEN.

- Do not use steam when ironing, as it may leave watermarks on the silk fabrics.

- See opposite page for suggested variations on this quilt theme.

- Before you begin, make sure the rotary cutter blade is ultra-sharp, as these fabrics need to be cut swiftly and cleanly to prevent any unnecessary fraying.

- Collect your fabrics and sort them into 'suits' and 'ties'. Cut out a number of 4½in (11cm) squares from each fabric and begin to lay them out in a simple repeating pattern (in my quilt the suit squares alternate with the tie squares), or in a random fashion if you prefer. Cut out more squares as you need them.

- If you want to make a quilt exactly the same size as the one pictured, you will need to cut out 104 silk squares and 104 wool squares, all 4½in (11cm) square, or a total of 208 assorted 4½in (11cm) squares – laid out with thirteen squares across and sixteen squares down.

- Lay out the fabrics so that the different designs are evenly distributed throughout the quilt top, and make adjustments so that you are happy with the arrangement before you begin sewing.

- Pick up the squares in rows (from left to right) or columns (from top to bottom, but begin from the left) in the order in which you will sew them, and label each row/ column with a number on a Post-It note pinned through the pile.

- Machine-piece the rows/ columns and press all seams open.

- Sew the rows/ columns together in the correct order to make the quilt top. Press all the seams open.

- Cut out the backing if using shirting, or make the backing if using narrower fabric (see Materials) using ½in (1cm) seams. The backing needs to be 3–4in (7.5–10cm) larger all around than the quilt top.

- Make the quilt sandwich (see page 142). Trim the edges so that the wadding and backing are 2in (5cm) bigger than the quilt top.

- This quilt looks lovely when hand-quilted with quite large running stitches in a contrasting thread. I created a criss-cross pattern with diagonal lines running through the 'suits' squares (not the 'ties' squares). Mark the lines with masking tape and remove it very gently when finished, as it can pull delicate silk threads.

- Trim the edges of the quilt with scissors or rotary cutter.

- Make and attach the binding (see page 143 for further instructions).

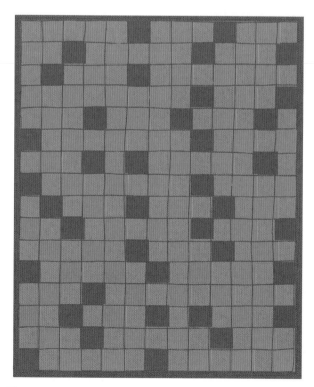

The quilt has thirteen squares across, and sixteen squares down.

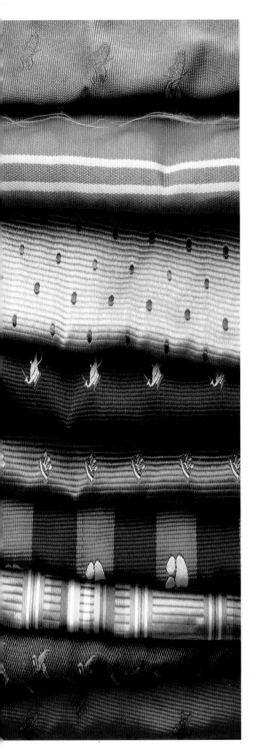

Variations on this theme

- Coats, blankets, skirts, suits, jackets and school uniforms are all good sources of wool fabric.

- Use tartan fabrics for a colourful effect.

- An all-woollen suit fabric quilt would look lovely if quilted with bright stitches, or hand-tied with a contrasting colour of wool (instructions for tying quilts can be found on the Internet).

- Wadding is not essential, as the wool fabric gives the quilt extra thickness. Or use a layer of wool fabric for the filling.

- Make a larger version for a sofa or bed to keep you really snug on winter nights.

- The surface of an all-wool or plain quilt offers a good opportunity to play with various types of stitching. Think of the way in which hand-quilters would often embellish monotone, plain or dark fabrics with lovely embroidery stitches such as herringbone, feather or cross stitch in contrasting and bright colours. For inspiration, look at traditional crazy patchwork; the best book on the subject is *Crazy Patchwork* by Janet Haigh (Collins & Brown, 1998).

- Like crazy patchwork, this type of quilt would also work well with a variety of fabric types such as silk, wool, cotton, satin, velvet, tweed, brocade, jacquard, Paisley and tartan, as well as embroidered fabrics.

- Rectangles could be used instead of squares – a good idea if you have only thin pieces of silk from old ties.

- The silk does not have to be tie silk – any lovely silk will do. It would be nice to use any leftovers from a Ball Gown quilt (see page 82) and thus have very luxurious his and hers quilts made from sumptuous fabrics.

hydrangea

This quilt is the expression of various inspirations, but mostly the deep blues and pinks of hydrangeas, a flower that runs through my life. When I was growing up, virtually every garden in our suburban neighbourhood had a solitary hydrangea, and even though these plants looked lonely, they added colour and interest to otherwise unspectacular planting. It wasn't until I spent many summers in Brittany and Normandy, where hydrangeas flourish in the mild, damp conditions, that I appreciated just how spellbinding they can be en masse. The gardens there don't have just one specimen but whole banks or even collections of them, and everywhere you look there are hydrangeas growing along roads, by walls and in hedges running down to the sea.

These days, the hydrangea is enjoying a renaissance in England as gardeners see beyond the basic blue and basic pink to the vast range of colours, shapes and habits. Places such as Trebah Gardens in Cornwall and the Savill Garden in Berkshire lead the way with stupendous plantings of all types of hydrangeas, which wind along in huge, colourful borders. These contain a beautiful palette of blues, from indigo to violet, and from lavender to china blue; and a wide range of pinks, from rose to wine red, and maroon to cerise; plus beautiful whites, creams and limes. There are plain hydrangeas, mop-heads and lace-caps, singles and doubles; hydrangeas that are weighty, delicate, cloud-like or star-like. Memories of these and all the lovely hydrangeas I have seen and admired here and abroad are stitched into this quilt.

The story began after I'd knitted some socks in deep, inky blue and green yarn and thought the same brilliant, vibrant colours would work in a quilt. I imagined splashes of Winsor & Newton inks in shades of viridian, cobalt, ultramarine, emerald and apple green. Then I found lots of suitable inky shades in fabrics such as the fabulous designs from the Kokka Coccinelle collection, with their slightly dusty, 'pricked', papery look and the stunning cobalt version of Philip Jacobs's 'Lilac Rose'. But no matter how hard I tried to get these to bond in an inky quilt, the colours simply would not work together well. So I removed the deep cobalts, bright turquoises and viridians, and then found I was left with a softer blue look, something that was more French, washed out and gentle, and this is how my hydrangea quilt came about.

design

I wanted this quilt to have a good mix of fabrics to create a fluid, non-geometric, 'bank of hydrangeas' effect, and I also wanted to be able to show off reasonably large sections of the lovely fabrics. I happen to think that small patterns are better in small pieces, but I discovered with this quilt that big prints can also be used to great effect in small squares. So I settled on a 4in (10cm) square (finished size), which is sufficiently large to show off whole small patterns and enough to capture interesting parts of larger patterns.

The latter fabrics were the real surprise: once I'd got into laying out the squares that I had cut from strips of large designs, I found that there could be up to three different styles of squares from the same fabric. For example, I obtained squares with lilacs, squares with

peach flowers, and squares with rich maroon roses – all from 'Lilac Rose' by Philip Jacobs. On the other hand, some squares from large-scale fabrics had to be left out when they fell in an area of the design with little interest. Using big prints in relatively small squares is a voyage of discovery, and mostly they did all the hard work; I did virtually no fussy-cutting except where I needed a square or two to finish a line.

After making the Postage Stamp quilt (see page 94), I was fascinated by the way that squares on point (square blocks set with the corners at north, south, west and east) give masses of energy and movement to a quilt, so decided to do the same here (but with bigger squares) and use squares on point set in vertical rows. I could perhaps have placed the squares on point in horizontal rows, but I find that with horizontal lines, the eye sometimes tires before it gets to the end of the row; whereas with vertical lines, the eye travels more comfortably down the channel or river.

The size of the quilt was dictated by the amounts of fabric available, and demonstrates my quilting philosophy nicely. There are twenty-one vertical lines, with thirteen squares in each. It was only when I had come to the end of my fabrics and laying out that I realized that there should be an even number of vertical lines if all four corners were to be the same. But as I had run out of fabric, I had to adjust the triangles to suit the corners. It goes to show that you can make this quilt with as many lines and squares per line as you like, as long as you are happy to play with the corners (I give instructions below).

I did not add a border because I wanted to replicate the way that hydrangeas billow and spill out and are allowed to grow as they like, and I wanted mine to grow right up to the edges of the quilt.

fabrics

When my first inspiration was thwarted and I saw that a deep, inky quilt wasn't going to work, I had to alter the choice of fabrics to suit the new gentle, calming feel of the quilt.

This is an indulgence quilt, an opportunity to use some of the fabrics I'd bought because I loved them, but for which I didn't have a specific purpose. It includes two (now rare) Kokka 'Coccinelle' blues bought in Purl Patchwork (see Resources, page 158) and a number of Rowan ones bought because I couldn't resist the aqua/ violet/ lime/ pink combination, plus a few older fabrics that have appeared in other quilts and here took on new nuances in different company. I chose rich colours with a pink and blue base, but avoided the bright blue and bubblegum pink of suburban hydrangeas and went instead for the dustier, deeper, richer, more unusual colours seen in special collections of plants.

I used ten fabrics in the squares, but as the 'Lilac Rose' designs cut up in different ways, it looks as though I've used more. My fabrics include: 'Begonia Leaves' (moss), two versions of 'Lilac Rose' (mint and natural), 'Geranium' (lime) and 'Grandiose' (taupe), all by Philip Jacobs, two Kokka 'Coccinelle' prints, 'Winding Floral' (green) and a hydrangea design from the Lille collection – both by Kaffe Fassett, and one fabric from the Utopia collection by Freespirit. The outer-edge triangles are in a 'Flea Market Fancy' fabric by Denyse Schmidt.

The same Utopia fabric appears on the back. This was chosen because it offered a surprisingly simple, stylized contrast to the densely flowered top, and it also picks out two of the main hydrangea colours.

The binding is made in a simple, deep leafy lime fabric that picks out the greens of the quilt and simply lets the design spread out, like real hydrangeas, rather than containing and framing it.

materials

Fabric suggestions: Decide on a colour theme and select fabrics that work harmoniously together – this is not a quilt with high contrasts. Instead of buying more individual fabrics, experiment with a couple of large-scale designs that will give you several styles of squares when cut carefully.

- - - - - - - - - - - - - - - - - - -

Quilt top: You will need an assortment of ten to twelve fabrics to a total of 4½yd/ m, with a minimum of 10in (25cm) of any single design. In my quilt, most fabrics appear twice so I would advise allowing for ½yd/ m of eight to ten fabrics and ³/₄yd/ m of any fabric likely to be used frequently.

Alternatively, work with numbers of squares required: cut out thirteen or any odd number of squares per row. My quilt has twenty-one vertical lines/ 273 squares, but a more correct version would have twenty-two vertical lines/ 286 squares.

You will need ½yd/m of fabric to make the side and corner triangles.

- - - - - - - - - - - - - - - - - - -

Backing: You will need 4³/₄yd (4.3m) fabric for the backing (I round up to 5yd/ 4.5m when buying, which also allows for a large repeat).

- - - - - - - - - - - - - - - - - - -

Binding: You will need 17½in (44.5cm) or ½yd/ m of fabric for the binding.

- - - - - - - - - - - - - - - - - - -

You will also need:

- A piece of wadding 3–4in (7.5–10cm) larger all around than the quilt top (I use 100 per cent organic cotton with scrim).
- 100 per cent cotton all-purpose sewing thread in ecru or taupe for the machine piecing.
- 100 per cent cotton quilting thread for machine- or hand-quilting.

- - - - - - - - - - - - - - - - - - -

Finished measurements: 61½ x 74½in (156 x 189cm).

directions

All seam allowances are ¼in (6mm) unless otherwise stated. Note that this quilt should be fully laid out before you begin sewing.

— Start by cutting out a pile of 4½in (11cm) squares from a width of each fabric. Place the squares in vertical rows 'on point' according to the diagram; as you go along, play with various fabric arrangements, introducing or taking out fabrics depending on how well they work. Once you are happy with the way the quilt is developing, cut out more 4½in (11cm) squares to make the quilt to your preferred dimensions (or follow the diagram).

— When all the squares are in place, cut out the triangles to go in the spaces. For this size of quilt, you will need to cut forty-two triangles for the edges. Cut out twenty-one 4⅞in (12.5cm) squares and cut these in two to make triangles.

— Cut the triangles for the corners. For the top corners, which are made up of two small triangles, cut two 4⅞in (12.5cm) squares into four half-triangles. For the bottom corners, which are one small triangle, cut one 3¾in (9.5cm) square into two half-triangles.

— If your quilt has an even number of both vertical and horizontal rows, or an uneven number of both, the four corner triangles will be the same.

— Pick up and piece the quilt according to the diagram (if you cannot leave the quilt out on the floor while you piece it, it is essential that you pick up the pieces in diagonal rows in the correct order, numbering them accordingly, so that there are no mistakes when piecing).

Putting the quilt together

Join strip 1 first, then the corner triangle (2), then strips 3, 4 and so on.

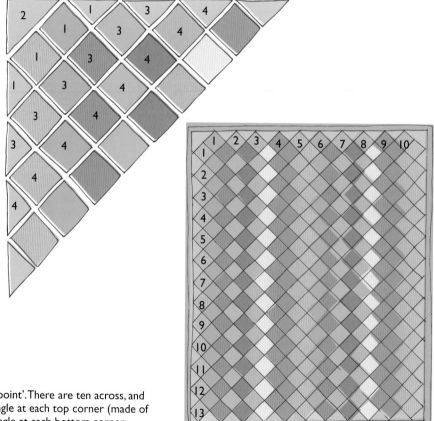

The quilt is made up of squares 'on point'. There are ten across, and thirteen down. There is a large triangle at each top corner (made of two small triangles), and a small triangle at each bottom corner.

- If you are new to piecing triangles, it can be a little tricky to get them right to begin with, so take some time at the start to work out how to get the seams to cross in the right places.

- Iron each row after piecing it, pressing the seams to the same side within each row, but alternate the direction row by row.

- Sew the diagonal rows together to make the quilt top. Iron and press the seams to one side. Trim the outside edge if preferred.

- Make the back by sewing together two widths of fabric with a ½in (1cm) seam allowance. The backing needs to be 3–4in (7.5–10cm) larger all around than the quilt top, so around 62 x 84in (157.5 x 213cm). Trim the excess fabric on both sides and then iron, pressing the central seam open.

- Make the quilt sandwich (see page 142 for further instructions).

- Trim so that the backing and wadding are approx. 2in (5cm) larger all around than the quilt top (unless you are having the quilting done professionally, in which case the wadding and backing should be 4in/ 10cm larger).

- Hand-quilt or machine-quilt. I used a deep violet thread and sewed horizontal lines of running stitches through the corners of the squares on every other row. The quilt would also look good with a grid of horizontal and vertical lines running through the squares (as in the Postage Stamp quilt, see page 94). Mark the lines with masking tape and remove gently when you have finished each one.

- Trim the edges of the quilt.

- Make and attach the binding (see page 143 for further instructions).

- Imagine yourself in a bower of beautiful blue hydrangeas.

russian
shawl

The two versions of this quilt were inspired by the visual memories of the time I spent in the former Soviet Union, both as a student and for work. These came flooding back when I looked at some fabrics I'd collected without quite knowing why I liked them so much – fabrics with huge, bright flowers in vivid pinks, yellows, oranges, viridians and reds on black backgrounds. They reminded me of the hand-painted lacquer boxes, the richly coloured shawls, and the traditional nested dolls known as *matryoshkas*, painted in brilliant hues, which were sold in souvenir shops. They also recalled a summer spent in the Ukraine, where the women wore simple dresses made with extravagantly floral cottons, and winter weeks spent in Moscow where the colours of the shawls, boxes and dolls stood out against drab skies and streets covered with dirty snow. They brought back memories of stories and novels about the indomitable Russian spirit, and the Russian love of gaiety, song and beauty.

More recently, I'd read *Russian Fabrics: Printed Cloth for the Bazaars of Central Asia* by Susan Meller (Abrams, 2007), which had photo after photo of exuberant – often red – cotton fabrics and it made me think that, even in the face of great difficulties, people still like to dress themselves in big prints in summer and wrap themselves in brilliant flowers in the winter.

The more I read and the more I looked at my fabrics, the clearer it became that they were destined to be Russian-inspired quilts. But what was the best design for them?

design

From the start, the design had to be big and bold to match both the scale of the fabrics and Russia's superpower status. I decided to combine the two main strands of inspiration – shawls and nested dolls – by making a square quilt that features squares within squares. In this way, the design turned into a huge Russian Log Cabin, rather like some of the super-sized, single-block quilts created by the quilters of Gee's Bend.

Of all the traditional American designs, the Log Cabin is my favourite. I like the way the block builds up from a central square, which in the past was often red to symbolize the home fire. There is something timeless and comforting about the idea of making a Log Cabin quilt to keep warm in cold North American winters, and I wanted to make a Russian version of the warming shawls that would be worn in snow-bound wooden houses in Russia.

My two quilts are a very simple single-block design, made by building up strips of fabric from a central square. I created contrast, though, by using two different widths of fabric and two types of fabric. There are thin strips in two-colour fabrics that alternate with the bolder floral patterns to give good, strong lines.

This is such a quick and easy design to make and suits all sorts of 'moods', not just Russian, that it is worth mastering the art of handling strips and making Log Cabin blocks (after all, you only have to make one block to make the whole quilt). It is a doddle to put together and makes a gloriously huge impact, because the simple design lets the fabrics do the hard work.

fabrics

I made the black Shawl version first, and was so pleased with the way it worked that I made a second version, Matryoshka, with the fabrics I'd collected but for which I couldn't find a vehicle.

Shawl version

I confess I have a passion for unsubtle fabrics. I particularly like florals on black backgrounds, and I had collected a few of these prints with no idea of how I would use them, as it was clear they would dominate anything other than an extravagantly dark and rich quilt. But, after contemplating them for a while, I saw that their designs were like the traditional, richly coloured square shawls that Russian women still wear. And, as with the shawls, I saw that the 'more is more' principle could apply, and they would look best like-with-like and en masse, and in this way evoke a classic Russian look.

There are six fabrics in this quilt: four florals and two fillers. The fabric in the central square and outermost wide band is 'Rose Divine' by Michael Miller. The enormous pink and red rose fabric in the second wide band is 'Rose Marie' by Michael Miller, and the two versions of the 'Chrysanthemums' design are from Timeless Treasures.

The thinner strips are made from Kaffe Fassett's Midnight 'Spots' (also the binding fabric) and Jennifer Paganelli's 'Casey Scroll'. The backing fabric is 'Flower Bed' from the Covent Garden collection from Benartex, which picks out the colours on the quilt top but doesn't fight with them.

Matryoshka version

Once I'd made the black Shawl quilt, I saw that the same design would suit another set of wickedly bright and very Russian fabrics that I had bought. There is nothing fey or subtle about them, I know, and although I had been attracted by the lacquer reds and viridians that reminded me of the colours used on many *matryoshka* dolls, I found them pretty challenging. But I was determined to get them into a quilt.

Again, the 'more is more' principle worked well and the more red and viridian I added, the better the whole thing looked. But I also think this quilt works because I kept to a strict colour code – I did try to introduce different shades of red and blue, but they looked terrible. Such bright, intense colours require a degree of confidence (because they are over-confident themselves), but in the end it's best to let them dictate how the quilt evolves. A repeating pattern also helped to create a balanced effect; this was necessary because the dark, Teal 'Geranium' would have stood out too much on its own and so had to be balanced with a second round. This is an unusual palette for me (I rarely use viridian, lacquer red, or teal), but it proved to me that fabrics that appear overwhelming and difficult at first can be used successfully.

I used three floral fabrics and two filler fabrics. The florals are Magenta 'Blowsey' (in the centre square, the outermost wide band and, stunningly, on the back), Scarlet 'Lilac Rose' (second wide band from the centre) and Teal 'Geranium' (in the first and third wide bands), which are all designed by Philip Jacobs. The two filler fabrics in the thinner strips are Green 'Spots' (also used for the binding) and Jade 'Silhouette Rose', both by Kaffe Fassett.

Left: Back of Shawl

Right: Shawl version

materials

Fabric suggestions: The eQuilter store has a great selection of huge and wildly coloured floral fabrics (www.equilter.com), including some stunners from Michael Miller and Timeless Treasures. You can use a different fabric per round or play with repeats. I admit I simply brought together my pieces of suitable fabrics (various lengths) rather than buying exact quantities. (There were some leftovers, but these will be used elsewhere.) You will need a maximum of five large floral fabrics, plus two or more fabrics to make the thinner bands.

Quilt top: You will need a large central square cut from ½yd/ m of fabric. My square was cut out as an 18½in (47cm) square (18in/ 45.5cm when finished); but if you have exactly half a yard, you could cut out an 18in (45.5cm) square.

When it comes to the quantities needed for the rounds, much depends on whether you use a different fabric per round or decide to repeat fabrics, so I am going to give requirements for each round.

For the wide floral bands, working out from the centre, you will need:

— First round: 16½in (42cm) of fabric

— Second round: 22in (55cm) of fabric

— Third round: 27½in (70cm) of fabric

— Fourth round: 33in (84cm) of fabric

For the thin bands: ½yd/ m fabric to make the first and third rounds, and just over ½yd/ m fabric to make the second and fourth rounds (either buy extra, e.g. ¾yd/ m, or buy ½yd/ m and use another similar fabric to make up the shortfall, as I have done in the Matryoshka quilt).

Backing: You will need 4½yd (4.1m) of fabric to make the backing.

Binding: You will need ½yd/ m of fabric to make the binding (add to the quantity required for the thin strips if using one of these fabrics).

You will also need:

— A piece of wadding 3–4in (7.5–10cm) larger all around than the quilt top (I use 100 per cent organic cotton with scrim).

— 100 per cent cotton all-purpose sewing thread in ecru or taupe for the machine piecing.

— 100 per cent cotton quilting thread.

Finished measurements 70 x 70in (178 x 178cm).

Left: Back of Matryoshka
Right: Matryoshka version

directions

All seam allowances are ¼in (6mm) unless otherwise stated.

— This is an ultra-easy quilt to make and one that grows quickly.

— As with any Log Cabin quilt, it is not possible to lay out the quilt exactly before sewing because you are dealing with long strips that are trimmed and then used again. However, I would recommend having a play with the fabrics before starting. Fold up fabric to make a central square, then place folded lengths of uncut fabric next to it to help decide which ones to use, and build up a general idea of the layout with uncut pieces.

— Once you have chosen the fabrics, start by cutting out the central 18½in (47cm) square.

— Then cut out the strips in two different sizes, cutting across the full width of each fabric. Cut 2in (5cm) strips for the 'in-between' bands, from the simple filler fabrics. Cut 5½in (14cm) strips for the wide bands and use the big floral fabrics.

— Cut out a few strips from each fabric, and cut out more as you go along. Trim the selvedges on each before sewing them together to make longer strips as necessary. Press each strip, opening out all the seams before sewing to the quilt top.

— The strips do not have to be exactly the right length, and can be longer than the sides to which they will be attached. After sewing to the side, trim the excess strip fabric with scissors or a rotary cutter and use the leftovers to make new strips.

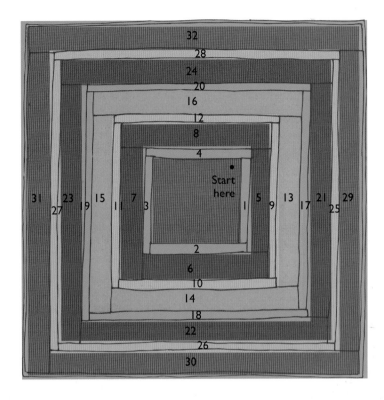

— The quilt is simply one huge Log Cabin block. Following the diagram above and beginning at the top right-hand corner, work in a clockwise direction adding strips to build up the square. Iron after sewing each new round, pressing the seams to one side. Note that you can make the quilt larger simply by adding more bands of fabric.

— When the quilt has reached the desired size, make the backing.

— If you are making the same size quilt as those shown here, you should make the backing by sewing together two full widths of fabric, 78in (198cm) long, with a ½in (1cm) seam (trim the selvedges first, if preferred). The backing should be 3–4in (7.5–10cm) larger all around than the quilt top.

— Make the quilt sandwich (see page 142 for further instructions) and trim the back and the wadding so that it is 2in (5cm) larger all around than the top.

— Machine- or hand-quilt. I used bright red thread and hand-stitched lines of simple running stitches next to the seam of each band (approx. ¼in/ 6mm away from the seam itself), starting on the inside edge of the central square.

— Trim the quilt top so that all the edges are even.

— Make and attach the binding (see page 143 for further instructions).

— Throw the quilt around your shoulders and dance the mazurka.

green,
green
grass
of home

This quilt takes its inspiration from two very ordinary garden features that inevitably make me think of home. First, there's the common-or-garden marigold, with its simple brightness and cheerfulness and its easy-going and easy-growing habit. As it happens, these pot marigolds (as they are also known) are at their best in May and June, which is also the time that the second inspirational garden feature, the grass, is richly emerald and full of little flowers that pop up everywhere. All this early summer colourful growth and exuberance inspired me to make a bright and happy marigold orange and grass green quilt.

As I sorted out possible fabrics, browsed for others to supplement my collection and wondered why there are so few truly, madly, deeply green fabrics available, a song kept playing in my head: 'The Green, Green Grass of Home', sung by Tom Jones. The record was released in 1966 and it was my very first favourite 'pop' song. I couldn't move when it was played on the kitchen radio – I had to stand still and concentrate on the music, and Tom's gravelly tones powerfully evoke a moment of loving home, a feeling that has remained with me all my life.

For me, green grass is symbolic of the outdoor space of home, but I am not a 'lawn fascist' as the garden writer Michael Pollan would say. In fact, like him, I am a 'lawn dissident' in that I prefer luxuriant, cushioning green grass with daisies growing to perfectly maintained, clipped, shorn lawns from which every dandelion and buttercup has been ruthlessly excluded. As a child I spent hours lying on soft grass, talking to friends or staring up at the sky or lying on my tummy revising for exams, and I can still recall the associated heat, smells and allergies, and the feel of cool blades of grass between my toes.

Marigolds, grass, memories and music combined to give me the idea, the colour scheme and the soundtrack for my quilt. When you have inspiration as deep-rooted as this, there only one thing to do. Quilt it.

design

I don't believe that simplicity of approach to making a quilt automatically equates to simplicity of final effect. We shouldn't undervalue simple, basic patterns and repeats with squares; these are 5in (12.5cm) squares (finished size) and the quilt builds up quickly, making it a perfect for a beginner.

My first idea with this quilt was to place the fabric squares in a random fashion, but this type of layout did not work and the result was uncoordinated and visually confusing. Then I remembered a quilt I'd seen years before in the American Museum in Bath. It was made up of squares set in diagonal lines: very simple, yet very effective.

So I picked up my squares and laid them out a second time in diagonal rows, and this time I was happy. The diagonal lines of fabrics lead the eye as if down garden paths. The fabrics work by having something – a colour or detail – that links each to its neighbour, so that the progression from one fabric to the next is natural and unstartling. If I screw up my eyes, it looks like a lawn or a patch of overgrown grass with interloping flowers.

My quilt has thirteen squares across and eighteen squares down, and I stopped when I'd filled up the available floor space on which I was working, a point that coincided – happily – with running out of fabric.

fabrics

I decided to make a colour story that focused on green as the background to bright, flowery colours so that the quilt would look like a wild meadow or an unruly back garden.

Deciding which shades of green to use was difficult, as there is a deficit of good green fabrics on the market. I didn't want limey or blue-greens, glaucous or pale greens, but truly grassy greens – something that is easier said than done. As a result, I had to collect my fabrics over quite a long period of time. I bought half-yards or half-metres of almost everything I thought I would want to include. In the case of this quilt, I could not get more than two long diagonal lines out of any one fabric, so I had to introduce more fabrics as necessary in the shorter lines.

The floral fabrics needed a very clear-cut design, with nothing blurry or watercolour-style, because I wanted the quilt to be in focus, not out of focus. I used seed packet and catalogue illustrations as my inspiration.

As well as oranges and greens, I found that buttery yellow chrysanthemums, rich red and pink carnations, lemony daffodils, rust coneflowers, gold sunflowers and bright little graphic flowers all worked. To these I added leafy and grassy prints in both Arts and Crafts and modern styles. My very favourite fabric is the one with the pale green gingham checked background, which looks like a flower-strewn picnic cloth.

I began with a limited number of fabrics because of the problem of finding luscious green designs, but the more I went through what I had gathered and what I had in my stock, the more possibilities I found. This was a timely reminder of the need for an open mind about what will work: you should never close off potential fabrics just because they appear not to work when stacked, as their dynamics will alter dramatically when they are cut. It's amazing how some very ordinary, uninspiring fabrics can cut up beautifully.

I used floral fabrics from the Flower of the Month series by Ro Gregg for Northcott (the carnation, chrysanthemum and rose), plus 'Persimmon' by Kaffe Fassett, 'Tall Hollyhocks' by Philip Jacobs, 'Coneflower' by Martha Negley and 'Sunflower' by Exclusively Quilters. The plainer greens are by Kaffe Fassett ('Stencil Carnation'), Denyse Schmidt (Katie Jump Rope collection) and Yuwa.

I decided to have a border on this quilt, because green grass in domestic gardens is usually enclosed by flowerbeds and borders. I wasn't sure which fabric to choose but the dark green 'Persimmon' print by Kaffe Fassett turned out to be the surprise in the mix; initially I didn't think such a dark fabric would work in the main body of the quilt, but in fact it acted as a glue, adding depth and harmony. It enclosed the flowery lawn like a hedge (it is similar in shade to yew or privet) to make the whole thing look like a suburban garden gone mad. Of course, it is possible to make the border wider or narrower, or to not have one at all if you prefer.

For the backing I decided that a simple design would work best, because anything big and blowsy would compete with the quilt top. I used a Kaffe Fassett spotty design with orange dots that could be construed as little marigold seedlings. This is a very large quilt, and two widths of fabric sewn together were not enough, so I added the strip of bright and startling chrysanthemums. This is a Flower of the Month fabric by Ro Gregg for Northcott.

I wanted the binding of the quilt to act as a firm, clear edge rather like the trimmed edge of a lawn, and used 'Little Wildflowers' by Heather Ross (from the Lightning Bugs collection) in a deep and rich corally-orange with a design of little blown-about flowers. I like the way this turned out: even though the binding is a darker orange than the oranges in the quilt, it works well with both sides.

♡ materials

Note

This design of quilt can be made to any size you like; part of the fun of making it is letting it grow to the dimensions that please you. So it works better if you take a flexible approach to fabric requirements, using an assortment of yards/ metres, half-yards/ half-metres and scraps rather than trying to calculate every last inch. Adjust the requirements for wadding, backing and binding if you alter the dimensions.

Quilt top: You will need a total of 6yd (5.5m) fabric to make the quilt top excluding the border. Use twelve to eighteen fabrics in pieces that are anything from scraps to half-yards/ half-metres – you will need at least ten to twelve of the latter.

A border is not essential and I would advise leaving your decision until you have the 'grass' section made and then matching the border to this. The border could be narrower or wider than mine, which is 7½in (19cm) wide (finished). You will need 2yd/ m of fabric for a border this size.

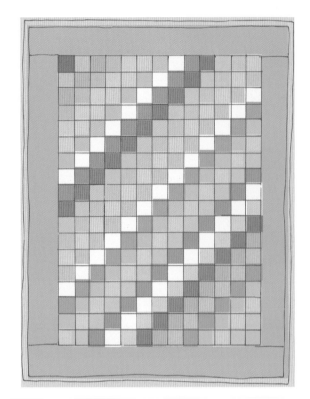

The quilt has thirteen squares across and eighteen squares down, plus a border. Add the two long side borders first, then the top and bottom borders. The prints are set in a diagonal pattern.

Backing: You will need 6yd (5.5m) of fabric for the backing PLUS a strip – 12 x 112in (30 x 284.5cm) – to extend it to the necessary width. This could be the same fabric or a second fabric. If you use a non-directional fabric such as spots, it's easy to cut this strip from widths of fabric, in which case add an extra yard/ metre to the quantity required.

Binding: You will need 22½in (56cm) of fabric. You can also make a binding with a mix of leftover fabrics – it doesn't have to be a single colour.

You will also need:

⌐ A piece of wadding 3–4in (7.5–10cm) larger all around than the quilt top (I use 100 per cent organic cotton with scrim).
⌐ 100 per cent cotton all-purpose sewing thread in ecru or taupe for the machine piecing.
⌐ 100 per cent cotton quilting thread.

Finished measurements: 80 x 104in (203 x 264cm), i.e. very large.

directions

All seam allowances are ¼in (6mm) unless otherwise stated.

— Begin by collecting the fabrics and playing with them. Gather together twelve to eighteen fabrics (I had eighteen possible designs and used sixteen, although one appears only as a single square in the corner and another in three squares). The pieces can be anything from scraps to half-yards/ half-metres and you will need at least ten to twelve of the latter.

— Keep an open mind at this point about what will and won't work, and do not commit to cutting out everything in one go. You can cut more squares as you go along and when you are able to see what works best.

— All squares need to be 5½in (14cm). Fussy-cut to get the centres of large blooms in a square if you like the effect (I do).

— Begin with small piles of squares and play with these to get a pleasing arrangement. Experiment with patterns and have a good time. Then cut out the rest of the squares.

— Clear a space on the floor and lay out the quilt. Once you are happy with the arrangement, pick up the squares either in rows or in columns, working from left to right. Number the piles of squares clearly with a Post-It note pinned to each stack.

— Piece the squares into long strips (horizontal if you have picked them up in rows, or vertical if you have picked them up in columns). Iron each row, pressing the seams to one side, and alternating direction with each row.

— Now sew together the rows or columns. Remember to begin sewing each seam from the end where you finished the previous seam. Don't sew in the same direction, e.g. from the top each time, because this may pull the rectangle out of shape, but work in an up-and-down direction. Iron again, pressing all the seams to one side (this time they can be in the same direction).

— If the quilt has a border, cut strips 8in (20cm) deep across the width of the fabric and sew these together to make longer strips for the four edges. Press the seams open. Sew the two longer borders to the sides first, and trim. Then sew the borders to the top and bottom. Iron, pressing the seams to one side.

— Iron the quilt top again, pressing the seams to one side (I press towards the outside edge all around).

— Make the backing by sewing together full widths of fabric using a ½in (1cm) seam, making sure it is 3–4in (7.5–10cm) larger all around than the quilt top. For a quilt this size, the backing needs to be 88 x 112in (223 x 284.5cm). Add an extra strip of fabric to make it wider if necessary. Press the seam(s) open.

— Make the quilt sandwich (see page 142 for instructions).

— Now it's time to quilt. Hand-quilt along the seams (about ¼in/ 6mm from the actual seam so that the needle isn't going through many layers) or in diagonal lines. I quilted with emerald green Mettler cotton quilting thread in diagonal lines, making a criss-cross pattern all over the quilt. Mark the lines to be quilted with masking tape by

running the edge of the tape through the corners of the squares. Take the running stitches right up to the edges of the border.

— After quilting, trim the edges of the sandwich with scissors or a rotary cutter. I don't mind slightly uneven edges; a gentle wonkiness can be hidden by the binding.

— Make and attach the binding (see page 143).

— Now all you have to do is lie on or under the quilt on the sofa or on the lawn, listen to Tom and luxuriate in the green, green grass of home – real, musical and textile.

amaryllis

I derive a huge amount of inspiration from the flowers I grow in the house and garden, and the name of this quilt tells you all you need to know about the driving force behind it. I have been growing amaryllises (more correctly known as hippeastrums) from bulbs for years, and they bring much-needed exotic colour and floral drama into the house during the dreary winter months. The enormous flowers are ridiculously easy to grow, and appear almost without fail even with minimal care and effort on my part, so I make sure I have a succession of huge blooms showing off on a window sill from November all the way through to May.

Amaryllises come in many gorgeous shades of deep red and rose pink, and *Hippeastrum* 'Benfica' is probably my favourite variety with its utterly stunning, deep, velvety, light-absorbing red blooms. It was this, together with the more unusual cybister hybrids such as *H.* 'Emerald', *H.* 'Ruby Meyer' and *H.* 'Exotic Star', with wonderful, intricate markings and stripes in combinations of reds and greens on strange-shaped petals, that inspired me to call this very red and green quilt my Amaryllis quilt.

The only trouble was that red and green can be something of a clichéd colour combination, one that many people associate with Christmas, and it was never my intention to make that type of quilt. Instead, this red and green quilt is based on very specific shades of these two colours, notably chartreuse and lime greens with cranberry and blood reds. I see a world of difference between these evocative colours and plain 'red and green'; it may be a matter of semantics for some, but I am unashamedly fussy about my colours. After all, they are a large part of what quilting is about.

So this quilt is a colourful indulgence, a way of celebrating and capturing, in a long-lasting textile, the rich colours of the beautiful flowers that brighten up the short, dark days of winter. It is no coincidence that I made it in January, when I had several amaryllises in bloom in terracotta pots; one

particularly miserable, cold day I suddenly decided to inject some colour into my life by starting a quilt, and needed to look no further than the flowers in the kitchen.

design

I spent a long time trying to see how to put the fabrics into a quilt so that it did not look like a classic Christmas quilt, and in the end decided that diamonds would be the ideal shape to display the jewel-like garnets, rubies and emeralds in the fabrics, despite the fact that I had never used this shape before. So I looked through a number of books for diamond-type inspiration and found plenty of very complex ideas which would have taken too long to make (including some stunning Lone Star quilts), but found all the inspiration I needed in two books: *Patchwork* by Kaffe Fassett and Liza Prior Lucy, and Kaffe Fassett's *Kaleidoscope of Quilts*. It took me a little while to master the art of cutting diamonds, but once I had done so, it was extremely satisfying to build up the diagonals and angles into a stained-glass window design. I used a diamond with a finished size of 5¼in (13.5cm) wide and 9in (23cm) long, but in fact the diamond could be any size (see box overleaf).

My quilt has nine diamonds down and twelve diamonds across, although to be more correct there should be an uneven number of diamonds (e.g. eleven or thirteen) running horizontally across the quilt so that the four corner triangles are the same. However, I ran out of fabric after making sets of twelve diamonds and could not justify extra fabric simply to make one more diamond per line. As a result, I had to make alterations to the corners and use two types of triangle instead of one. But no one has ever noticed the differences in the corners and I am pleased that I resisted spending more money on fabric just to get the quilt 'right' when I had already got the result I wanted.

cutting diamonds

This type of quilt can be made with any size of diamond, and can be built up with as many diamonds as you like, according to quantities of fabric available. It works best with rows made up of an odd number of diamonds across and down, but if you find that you run out of fabric, you can stop and fill in the outside edge spaces with triangles. There are two ways of cutting out diamonds: using a template or a quilting ruler.

Using a template

Make your own template(s) with firm cardboard or template plastic (available from quilting shops and websites), or buy a ready-made template. Download diamond shapes from the Internet, or photocopy templates, or create your own size and shape of diamond. The diamond used to make this quilt is 5¾in (14.5cm) wide and 10in (25cm) long (cut size, before sewing).

Using a quilting ruler

It is quite straightforward to cut out diamonds using the angle lines on a quilting ruler. There are some excellent diamond-cutting tutorials on the Internet. I recommend the simple and easy technique shown on www.quilting.about.com (see http://quilting.about.com/od/rotar ycuttingskills/ss/cutting_shapes_6. htm) but if you do a search for instructions for cutting diamonds and triangles, you will find plenty.

You will then need to cut the necessary triangles to fill in the gaps and corners, and the directions for these can be found on the same Internet pages as for diamonds, in Liza and Kaffe's books (see page 71), or in general quilting handbooks. You need four different triangles: tall triangles for the spaces along the top and bottom edges, wide triangles for the spaces along the sides, and two small and two large triangles for the corners.

✂ fabrics

As this quilt is all about colour, I had a ball choosing the fabrics. This is a real feel-good, lift-the-spirits quilt to put together and I would urge anyone who has a much-loved colour theme, colour combination or palette to have a go at making a quilt that expresses their passion. However, because I was so specific about the shades of red and green, it took some time and a great deal of sorting before I had enough to create the effect I wanted; that is, for the colours to meld and run into each other, to create the impression of walking into a conservatory or greenhouse full to bursting with masses of pink, red and green amaryllis blooms all grouped together. It also took several days to complete the layout, as I worked very slowly, building up the lines, and tried out quite a few fabrics that then had to be rejected because they did not fit into the very narrow colour palette.

Unfortunately, there are no actual amaryllis flowers in the quilt, but there are plenty of greenhouse or hothouse tender plants such as dahlias, morning glories and geraniums. There are also some stunning red edibles such as ruby-red vegetable leaves and plums, plus a variety of garden flowers such as foxgloves, roses and marigolds. There are

fourteen fabrics in all, including four by Philip Jacobs (Red 'Foxgloves', Red 'Luscious', Magenta 'Morning Glory' and Tobacco 'Geranium', two by Kaffe Fassett ('Minton' and 'Burnt Rose') and four Martha Negley prints variously featuring plums, vegetable leaves, chrysanthemums and dahlias. There is one Japanese red and cream rose fabric from Kokka, and three contrasting off-white and green leafy prints from the Kokka Coccinelle collection, with exactly the right shade of chartreuse that works so well with the reds.

The backing is made with the Philip Jacobs 'Morning Glory' design. The shop didn't have quite enough, but as the piece I bought was only a few inches short, I lengthened it with two strips of leftover fabric – and this gives added detail to the back. The same happened with the binding; again I added a strip of a different fabric to make the binding go all the way round. And if you look very carefully, you will see that there is something of a mish-mash of the three green Japanese fabrics in the outside triangles, and one of the lines of diamonds contains three different red designs due to the fact that I was using up what was left over rather than making a perfect quilt.

I hand-quilted in red thread along the diagonal seams – it was not necessary to do any fancy quilting, as the 'busyness' of the top did not need any extra detail.

materials

Quilt top: My quilt measures 63½ x 81in (162 x 206cm) and uses fourteen fabrics in total.

A 10in (25cm) length of fabric 42in (106cm) wide will give twelve diamonds measuring 5¾in (14.5cm) wide and 10in (25cm) long if you cut using a template, so it is simple to calculate how much fabric you need, provided you are happy for there to be an even number of diamonds in each horizontal row when technically there should be an uneven number (see box on page 72). If not, buy extra fabric. For the 108 diamonds in the quilt, you need at least 2½yd/ m fabric. For the eighteen triangles for the sides, top and bottom, you need 11in (28cm) fabric. For the rectangles to make the corner triangles, you need another piece of fabric at least 6⅛ x 16½in (15.5 x 42cm).

To make the triangles, cut as follows. Ten tall triangles for top and bottom: cut five 6⅜ x 11in (16.25 x 28cm) diamonds across widthways into two triangles. Eight wide triangles for sides: cut four 6⅜ x 11in (16.25 x 28cm) diamonds lengthways into two triangles. Two small triangle corners: cut one 3½ x 6in (9 x 15cm) rectangle in half diagonally to make two triangles. Two large triangle corners: cut one 6⅛ x 10½in (15.5 x 26.5cm) rectangle in half diagonally to make two triangles.

However, I began by simply collecting/ buying fabrics in half-yard or half-metre pieces and adding any suitable fabrics from my collection as long as there was sufficient to make a full row of diamonds (in my case, this is twelve). It is possible to use a different fabric for each row or have repeats of fabrics. For example, I used the 'Geranium' fabric in three rows, because it was a key fabric and I had half a yard of it. I also used 5yd/ m of fabric for the backing and ½yd/ m of fabric for the binding.

lisbon
tile

Once upon a time, a long time ago, I was a European brand manager for Malibu, the well-known drink. My work entailed travelling all over Europe, and one of my very favourite places to visit on business was Portugal, especially Lisbon, but I never had time to wander round the city at leisure, and knew I was missing something special.

I wanted to remedy this and recently spent a few May days in Lisbon and cannot recommend the city highly enough for anyone who likes flower shops that spill on to mosaic-patterned pavements, vivid lilac jacaranda trees in old squares, rattling vintage yellow trams, 1930s buildings in ice-cream colours, haberdasheries that haven't changed in decades, time-warp cafés where they serve wonderful coffee and not-to-be-missed *pastéis de nata* (custard tarts).

Lisbon is unusual in that it has a fascinating jumble of architectural styles; where other cities have pulled down and rebuilt, Lisbon has developed in a more organic, laissez-faire manner so that the place is full of interesting details from all sorts of periods, including several that are rarely seen in Europe, such as the 1940s and 1960s, as well as the more usual nineteenth-century, art deco, Moderne and contemporary. And everywhere you look, you find tiles (*azulejos* in Portuguese). They are on exterior walls and interior walls, in panels, in gardens and squares, cafés, shops and restaurants, and are an unparalleled source of quilting inspiration.

Typically they are painted in fresh, breezy Atlantic colours of blue and white, but there are also many that add sea greens and aquas, sandy golds and earthy browns. My favourites were the tile panels on the outside of buildings that look like permanent, washable quilts and which reflect the huge variety of artistic and architectural styles and movements. These consist mostly of one type of tile set in traditional geometric patterns, but there are also some fantastic panels from the second part of the twentieth century,

which are made from more abstract, expressionist and even groovy (think 1970s pop art) tiles. No matter what the style, though, each panel is a wonderful lesson in quilt patterning, the joys of repetition, and in covering a surface with artist-made squares.

The tiles of Lisbon could inspire a whole book of quilts (you have only to look at *Tile Designs from Portugal* by Diego Hurtado de Mendoza, published by The Pepin Press in 2007, to see the vast number of possibilities), but I had to restrict myself to one, which then became two when I saw how many tile-inspired fabrics are to be found in shops and on websites. Tiles, it seems, are one of the best traditional and cultural inspirations a quilter – or any pattern-maker – could hope for.

design

This was one of the easiest designs to create. As well as looking at them *in situ*, I'd also taken lots of photos of tiled panels in Lisbon for future reference, and it was clear from these that my quilt had to be a rectangle filled with squares or 'tiles', and perhaps with some sort of border, because this is the most common panel pattern.

I started off by cutting out my 5½in (14cm) squares (sometimes fussy-cutting to get the best part of a tile pattern into the square) and laying them out randomly. At this point I was so delighted that there was such an abundance of tile-themed fabrics available

that I didn't see the need for a repeat pattern. However, the huge number of fabrics was a hindrance rather than a help, and the initial layouts simply did not work and flow. Then I realized that this quilt wasn't meant to flow and was never going to flow because so many of the fabric squares are self-contained, tile-like patterns which only really achieve a good effect when they are repeated.

So I picked up the squares and started again, this time with a 'four-patch' block (a block made up of four equal squares), in this case using two squares each of two fabrics. But even this did not work happily because the colours were not looking good, despite the fact that I had bought them to fit into a certain palette (see Fabrics, right). Eventually, I saw that, although the fabrics looked lovely all stacked up together in a pile, there was too much of a range between the dark and the light for them to work well in a quilt. So I decided to make two separate panels: one pale, more twentieth century, with a mix of geometric and abstract patterns in soft aquas, blues and yellows, and the other dark, more traditional, with classic tile patterns in deeper browns, greens and turquoises.

I then linked the pair by making them mirror images of each other: the pale quilt has a dark inner border made from some of the fabrics used in the dark quilt, which in turn has a pale inner border. I also added an outer border to each made of rectangles (the equivalent of two squares or 'tiles') to create extra visual interest.

fabrics

The fabric selection for this quilt was dictated entirely by the central idea of tiles. I was completely spoilt for choice, but managed to narrow my options by adhering to what I consider to be a fairly typical Portuguese palette (blues, yellows, green, turquoises). I found around twenty-five fabrics with no difficulty at all – tile-based designs abound in shops and on websites such as eQuilter (www.equilter.com), and I chose a mix of regular, traditional designs and abstract modern designs. However, I could have found enough fabrics to make many more colour stories and patterns, and if you like the idea of a tile quilt but have a different source of inspiration, I am sure you will have no difficulty finding fabrics to make different versions of this quilt (it could be done in black and white/ terracotta/ marble colours).

In my selection I included fabrics from the following collections and designers: the Midwest Modern 2 collection by Amy Butler (who designs many spectacular 'tile' fabrics), 'Ava Rose' by Tanya Whelan, 'Sun Drop' by Dena, the Sis Boom Basics collection by Jennifer Paganelli (who also designs more great 'tile' fabrics), 'Chestnut Hill' by Joel Dewberry, 'Alhambra' by Art Gallery Fabrics, and 'Ginger Blossom' and 'Andalucia' from Michael Miller.

I also wanted the backings to continue the tile theme. The backing on the pale quilt is 'Tiled Primrose' by Heather Bailey, a sweet, small-scale, regular pattern in summery Portuguese sea and sun hues. The dark quilt backing is made from the huge, 1970s-style 'Pop Daisy' from the Pop Garden collection, also by Heather Bailey. I then extended the twin/ mirror image idea by using the 'Tiled Primrose' for the binding of the dark quilt and the 'Pop Daisy' for the binding of the pale quilt.

materials

Notes

- This pattern makes a smallish quilt that would be good on a chair, small bed, or on back of a settee. However, it is possible to enlarge the design by adding more four-patch blocks. It is not essential to have a border.
- This quilt would make a good single bed quilt. If you want to enlarge it, buy the fabrics in half-yard/ half-metre pieces and make more four-patch blocks, adjusting the wadding, backing and binding accordingly.
- The pale version contains twelve fabrics plus two contrasting fabrics in the thin strips, which were left over from dark version. The dark version has fifteen fabrics in the squares plus one fabric in the border which was left over from the pale quilt.

Fabric suggestions: A collection of tile-themed designs is ideal. This is a great quilt for leftovers, as the minimum amount needed of any fabric is two 5½in (14cm) squares, and you can include as many designs as you like. Alternatively, buy a selection of ten to twelve fabrics in a similar colour palette and a contrasting fabric for the inner border.

Quilt top: To make a quilt this size, you will need a third of a yard/ metre each of ten to twelve fabrics, or a selection of fabrics up to a total of 4yd (3.6m). If you have full widths of all the fabrics, this will also be enough for the corner squares and the rectangles for the outer border.

Contrasting inner border: You will need ½yd/ m of fabric for this.

If using leftovers and a mixture of fabric pieces, you need enough for eighty-four 5½in (14cm) squares (main panel and outer border), twenty 5½ x 10½in (14 x 26.5cm) rectangles (outer border), four short strips 2½ x 5½in (6 x 14cm) for the extension of the inner border, plus four long strips for the inner border – two 2½ x 44½in (6 x 113cm) and two 2½ x 50½in (6 x 128cm).

Backing: For the backing, you will need 4yd/ m of fabric. The leftovers will give enough to make the binding, too, if you want to use the same fabric. Allow for a little extra length if using a pattern with a large repeat.

Binding: You will need 15in (38cm) of fabric to make the binding (if you are not using leftovers from the backing).

You will also need:

- A piece of wadding 3–4in (7.5–10cm) larger all around than the quilt top (I use 100 per cent organic cotton with scrim).
- 100 per cent cotton all-purpose sewing thread in ecru or taupe for the machine piecing.
- 100 per cent cotton quilting thread.

Finished measurements: 54 x 62½in (137 x 158.5cm).

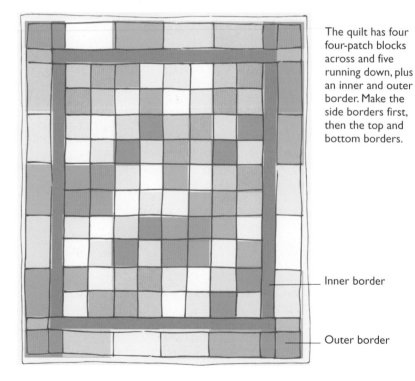

The quilt has four four-patch blocks across and five running down, plus an inner and outer border. Make the side borders first, then the top and bottom borders.

Inner border

Outer border

directions

All seam allowances are ¼in (6mm) unless otherwise stated

- Begin by cutting out eighty 5½in (14cm) squares for the main panel in a mixture of fabrics. You may prefer to cut out eight squares from ten fabrics, or you may simply want to cut out multiples of two squares from some of the fabrics you think may work, and then cut out more when you are happy that they will work. A fabric does not have to be with the same partner each time.

- Now lay out the squares in four-patch blocks (see diagram) for the main section. There should be four blocks across and five blocks down, unless you are making a larger/ smaller quilt.

- When you are happy with the layout, pick up the squares row by row or column by column (if you are unable to leave the squares out until you have finished piecing, pick up the squares by row and label each pile with a number so that you know what goes where).

- Iron each row/ column and press the seams to one side, alternating direction with each row/ column.

- Then sew the strips of squares together to make the quilt top. Iron and press the seams to one side.

- Alternatively, begin by making twenty four-patch blocks and then lay these out; sew them together to make the central panel.

- Now cut out and sew on the inner borders, which should be cut from a contrasting fabric or fabrics. Start with the sides, and make two strips 2½in (6cm) wide and 50½in (128cm) long. Sew these to either side of the quilt top. Iron, pressing the seams to one side. Then cut out the strips for the top and bottom inner border. Cut out two strips 2½in (6cm) wide and 44½in (113cm) long, and sew to the top and bottom edges. Iron, and press the seams to one side.

- Make the outer border and corners. You will need: eight short strips, 2½ x 5½in (6 x 14cm) to go next to the corner squares – these can be in the same contrasting fabric(s) as the inner border (dark version) or in a fabric or fabrics in the main panel (pale version); four 5½in (14cm) squares for the corners; twenty rectangles 5½ x 10½in (14 x 26.5cm) for the outer border.

- Lay out these pieces according to the diagram. Create the two side borders by making strips with a square then a short strip, four rectangles, a short strip, and a square. Iron, pressing seams to one side. Sew the borders to the sides, making sure all seams are aligned, and press again.

- Make the top and bottom borders by making two strips (square, short strip, four rectangles, short strip and square). Sew to the top and bottom edges and iron. The quilt top is now finished.

- Make the backing by sewing together two widths of backing fabric 70in (178cm) long. Join with a central ½in (1cm) seam and press the seam open. The back should be 3–4in (7.5–10cm) larger all around than the quilt top.

- Make the quilt sandwich (see page 142). Trim so that the wadding and backing are 2in (5cm) larger all around than the quilt top.

- Machine- or hand-quilt. I used a pale aqua thread and hand-quilted with simple running stitches using the seam lines as guidance. I stitched lines along horizontal seams (about ¼in/ 6mm) and all round the border.

- Make and attach the binding (see page 143 for further instructions).

- Get a cup of coffee or a glass of Portuguese wine and imagine yourself on the sunny terrace of a tile-clad café in Lisbon.

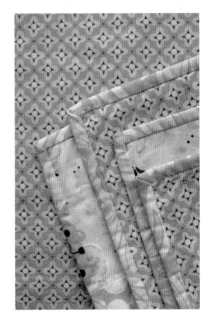

ball
gown

This is a quilt that elicits lots of 'oohs' and 'aahs' and yet it's incredibly quick and easy to make. The inspiration came from a photo I saw about ten years ago in a magazine, of a strikingly simple, yet stunningly effective silk quilt. It was casually but elegantly thrown on a simple camp bed and was made up of large squares of brightly coloured silks with contrasting thick handstitching. This was in the days before I began quilting, and I looked and looked at this quilt as if to convince myself that, yes, of course I could make one. Eventually, after about three or four years, I took myself off to the fabric shops of Berwick Street in London's Soho to look for some vivid silk dupion and had a lovely time choosing all my favourite bright colours (gold, garnet, violet, lime, cerise, plus a silvery grey) and making my quilt.

Over the years, I've often thought about making another silk quilt. Then, one day, after seeing some particularly beautiful silk fabrics, I fell to musing about all the gorgeous dresses that can be made out of plain, shot and embroidered silks: prom dresses, wedding dresses, bridesmaids' dresses, cocktail dresses and, of course, ball gowns – and felt newly inspired.

First I toyed with the idea of an ivory/pastel embroidered and beaded creation. However, I decided that although this would be very lovely, it would probably be too pale for my taste (plus beaded silks are prohibitively expensive). So then I went back to my passion for colour, and decided to use fabrics that could be used in the ball gown of my dreams, the kind of garment that would be waiting for Cinderella when her Fairy Godmother announces that 'You shall go to the ball', the kind of fantasy dress I might secretly wish was hanging in my wardrobe just waiting for the invitation to the ball to arrive. And this is how my Ball Gown quilt came about.

design

The design is ultra-simple and the quilt is made up of generously large squares. (There is also a practical element to this choice of design: silk frays badly and larger pieces are easier to handle.) When deciding on the size of the squares, I was guided by what could be cut most economically from half-yard/half-metre pieces. Because most fabrics are sold with an extra inch or so, it's often possible to cut out two strips of 10in (25cm) squares, which give eight squares per half-yard. (If you find your half-yard really is a half-yard, you may need to reduce the size of the squares.) The quilt squares can be any size; I chose to cut 10in (25cm) squares because I wanted the quilt to grow quickly and have a big impact.

I liked the original magazine quilt, with its random, no-repeat pattern design, and decided to copy this, although a two-colour or repeated pattern could look good. The trick with so-called 'random' placing is to make your first layout quickly and instinctively, then to stand back and look at it critically before making adjustments. The effect should be like scattered jewels or a rustling, swishing ball gown that gleams and glitters in the light.

fabrics

I bought all the fabrics for the quilt top in one go from Broadwick Silks in London, a wonderful, ethereal silk emporium on Broadwick Street, a short side street off Berwick Street, with its contrastingly down-to-earth fruit and veg market. On my first visit, I wandered round and round the bolts of silk dupion, trying to decide on a colour scheme. With the help of the very enthusiastic and creative assistant (the shop staff here are very well qualified: some are designers or MA students, and most have fashion and/ or textiles degrees), I pulled out a sumptuous range of gold and turquoise fabrics – but nothing embroidered. She then made me an incredibly useful fabric swatch for reference and off I went to think about it.

A week later, I decided that the reversible fabric I'd initially chosen was just a little too 'upholstery' for me and I went back to the shop to see if there was anything I liked better. My eyes were immediately drawn to the fabrics with lots of surface machine embroidery and eventually I picked one I thought would make a seriously lovely ball gown – and worked from there. I knew the quilt had to be in rich colours because I wanted my Cinderella to stand out in the crowd, and with the help of the assistant (just as delightfully enthusiastic as the first) pulled out all the pinks, golds and oranges to go with the embroidered silk – and then added another embroidered silk for good measure. We also included a fabulously glamorous (think Ava Gardner) metallic gold fabric to make the whole thing look even more glittering. If it really were a dress, it would be just the thing for an autumn ball.

Deciding on the backing fabric was great fun. I didn't want anything too plain or too small because this is a quilt to smack the eyes, so I went for the gloriously enormous 'Garden Party' design in Coral by Philip Jacobs, because it's not often you can use such huge prints and exploit their full size to great effect. (Note: I did consider a silk backing, but decided against it, as a silk-backed quilt will slide off a bed or furniture at the slightest movement.)

I had thought that a binding in purply silk fabric would create a nice contrast, but decided that handling a thin strip of silk that long would lead to nothing but tears, so instead chose a cotton leaf fabric in rich autumnal colours and touches of green (this is 'Garden Maple' by Michael Miller), which adds a nice touch of interest around the outside.

For the style of hand quilting, I decided to keep to the original photo that inspired the quilt and to create lines of large running stitches using three strands of DMC embroidery cotton. However, I didn't have enough of any one colour and was loath to buy more when I had plenty of thread in other colours, so decided to use a variety including golden yellow, coral, pink and taupe, colours that either matched or contrasted with the silks.

materials

Fabric suggestions: I planned this quilt carefully because of the cost of some of the fabrics. However, in the UK dupion silk is in fact the same price per yard/ metre as cotton quilting fabric (embroidered and metallic silks cost more).

- - - - - - - - - - - - - - - - - -

Quilt top: You will need 5yd/ m of silk fabric. My quilt was made from ten fabrics bought in half-yard/ half-metre pieces. If you want to make a larger quilt to cover the whole of a king-size bed, you should allow 6yd/ m (and increase the quantities for backing, wadding and binding).

- - - - - - - - - - - - - - - - - -

Backing: You will need 5¼yd/ m of fabric PLUS a strip of fabric 12 x 84in (30 x 213cm) to enlarge the backing to the full width of the top, plus 3–4in (7.5–10cm) extra allowance (you can make this by cutting two strips, 12in/ 30cm wide, across the width of the fabric). The strip can be the same fabric as the main part of the backing or a contrasting fabric.

- - - - - - - - - - - - - - - - - -

Binding: You will need 20in (51cm) fabric to make the binding .

- - - - - - - - - - - - - - - - - -

You will also need:

- A piece of wadding 3–4in (7.5–10cm) larger all around than the quilt top (I use 100 per cent organic cotton with scrim).
- 100 per cent cotton all-purpose sewing thread in ecru or taupe for the machine piecing.
- Cotton embroidery thread (e.g. Anchor or DMC), silk embroidery thread or 100 per cent cotton quilting thread for hand quilting.

- - - - - - - - - - - - - - - - - -

Final measurements: 86in wide x 76½in long (218.5 x 194cm).

directions

Notes before you sew silk

Working with silk is a lot trickier than working with well-behaved quilting cottons. Silk is slippery and prone to fraying, so handling needs to be kept to the minimum. The key to using silk is to treat it carefully, work quickly, and try not to pull/ drag/ touch the edges at all.

Do not pre-wash silk fabrics (most of them are dry-clean only). You may not even have to iron them unless they are horribly creased, because they flatten very easily under the pressure of the ruler as you work. Do not steam-iron silk as it can leave watermarks on the fabric.

Embroidered silk fabrics stretch markedly after cutting because the fabric was previously held by the machine stitches – so you need to use the edges of the non-stretchy silk as your sewing/ matching guidelines.

There is no way of preventing fraying, especially along the long outside edges; just exercise care when handling, grit your teeth and work as quickly as possible. I did everything from laying out to sewing up the whole quilt top in a day, because I didn't want to spend too long picking up and putting down the unfinished pieces. So in fact it's a very quick quilt to make (imagine you are Cinderella's Fairy Godmother with only a day to make her ball gown).

I don't trim the fraying threads, because I find shorter threads lead to more fraying.

Take care to keep all the loose threads on the wrong side when sewing up.

The quilt has nine squares across and eight squares down.

Make sure the rotary cutter blade is very sharp (use a new one if necessary), because it's really important to cut the squares as swiftly and cleanly as possible to avoid any unnecessary fraying.

Some people prefer to use a ½in (1cm) seam allowance when working with silk because of the problem with fraying (in which case, I would have cut out 10½in/ 26.5cm squares). Consider this if you are new to sewing silk.

— Cut out the squares. The squares can be any size you like, but mine are 9½in (24cm) finished size, 10in (25cm) when cut. The size of the square may be dictated by the amount of fabric in your half-yard/ -metre pieces.

— Cut out about half of each colour of fabric and then begin to play with the layout until you are happy with it. Then cut out more squares in batches.

— I laid out nine squares across and eight squares down, so the quilt covers a double bed or a settee. But you can arrange the layout of squares to suit your taste/ bed/ settee (but do take this into account when buying wadding, plus backing and binding fabric).

— Be aware that different lights produce very different visual effects with silk, so try to look at the layout in various lights. Sunlight creates a wonderful shimmer and picks up the different colours in shot silks, but I had to pull down the blind/ close the curtains so that I could check the colours (it was very difficult to tell the golds and the pinks apart in the sunshine).

— You may want to create a pattern or have a 'random' layout like mine, in which case make sure that fabrics

are scattered throughout and that there aren't any unintentional repeats. Now you are ready to sew.

— Pick up each row across or column down and machine-piece together to make a strip of squares. Number each row/ column with Post-It notes pinned through the pile before you sew it, and reattach the labels after sewing.

— Gently iron each strip, pressing the seams to one side, alternating the direction of the seams with each strip (e.g. odd rows down and even rows up). DO NOT use steam, as it can leave watermarks on the fabrics.

— Now machine-sew the strips together in the correct order to make the quilt top.

— Press the new seams to one side – this time they can all be ironed in the same direction.

— Make the backing by sewing together two full widths of fabric, 84in (213cm) long. If you make the same size quilt as the one here, you need to make the backing wider by adding a strip of fabric 12 x 84in (30 x 213cm). This can be the same

fabric or a contrasting fabric. It should be 3–4in (7.5–10cm) bigger all around than the quilt top.

— Make the quilt sandwich (see page 142 for more information).

— Decide how you are going to hand-quilt. I quilted a simple grid pattern using the seams as guidelines, but you could do a criss-cross pattern, or work round the inside of squares, or intersect each square with a line. Use bold stitches and a contrasting colour (or colours) to create a lovely hand-embroidered effect. I used three strands of DMC cotton embroidery thread in a variety of colours.

— Trim the edges carefully, cutting off frayed threads. I left pins in around the outside squares to hold the silk in place and to stop further fraying until I was ready to attach the binding.

— Attach the binding (see page 143).

— Now you shall go to the ball.

floral
frocks

As someone who dreams of wearing nipped-in, full-skirted dresses flaunting an entire herbaceous border's worth of summer flowers, I did not want to miss the fabulous exhibition of floral frocks at the Fashion Museum in Bath a couple of years ago. 'The Pick of the Bunch' was, very simply, a celebration of the floral printed dress, the staple of the summer wardrobe for so many women in the twentieth century. But it was not just the designs that were wonderful – some exuberant, some restrained, some feminine and others very sophisticated – but also the fabrics within them. Together they made the ultimate, girly, attractive, summer fashion statement, and one that has, happily, made a return to High Street shops in recent seasons.

There is an undeniable joy in wearing cool, fresh, pretty cotton dresses in summer. I imagine most women have memories of a favourite summer dress and can recall the details exactly: the design and fabric pattern, any smocking or ribbons, collar or buttons, the way it gathered at the waist or tied at the back. My childhood favourite was fresh yellow with a wide sash that I used to learn to tie my first bows. It was sleeveless and gathered at the waist and I could do a lovely twirl in it. It flew up when I rode my bike and came down like an umbrella when I hung upside down from the crossbar of our swing.

The exhibition reminded me of the beauty of floral cotton fabrics, the sort of fabrics we simply don't see today except in quilt shops. Once, you could walk into any fabric shop or department store and be spoilt for choice with gorgeous flowery cottons – and now there's next to nothing. But step inside a quilt shop and you will find all sorts of floral beauties. I have often thought that it would be possible to make clothes out of them, but as I don't have the dressmaking skills, I decided instead to make a Floral Frocks quilt with the pick of the quilt fabric bunch.

I wanted to make something that captured the sheer pleasure of wearing fabulous floral frocks, something that encapsulated warm sunny days, balmy evenings, bare legs, seaside holidays and classic English summers.

Although daintier flowers would work well in such a quilt, I liked the exuberance, the loudness and the botanical realism of so many of the frock fabrics in the exhibition. So this quilt reflects the dresses I liked most, those of the late 1940s and 1950s, with Dior-style 'New Look' full skirts and tight-fitting waists that rejected wartime austerity with a 'frivolous' use of fabric and offered much-needed ideas of romance and femininity.

fabrics

I knew that I wanted very clear and graphic flowers like the ones used on vintage dress fabrics (and not the type of flowers that appear on furnishing textiles – see the style of the Charming Chintz quilt, page 130, for an illustration of what I mean). When, on a chance visit to Quilters' Haven in Suffolk, I discovered the Flower of the Month fabrics by Ro Gregg for Northcott, I knew I had exactly what was required. Delightfully, they feature flowers that have delicate fragrance, too, such as roses and lily of the valley. It's so easy to imagine young women wearing generous skirts and waist-enhancing dresses made from these fabrics, with a cotton cardigan for cool days.

Pink and green, for me, is the ultimate English summer combination: it's fresh, pretty, cool and very 'English rose'. Pinks and greens can be found all over England in June and July: in roses, peonies, snapdragons and hollyhocks, all set off to perfection by various shades of green foliage. Although I bought six fabrics, I only used four floral designs in the quilt because I wanted to keep it simple and striking (the two rejected fabrics detracted from the very clean pink/ white/ green palette) so I used one May/ Lily of the Valley fabric and three June/ Rose fabrics.

Even if you cannot find these exact fabrics, there are so many fantastic floral prints to inspire a frock quilt that a quilter is spoilt for choice (eQuilter has a brilliant selection: see Resources, page 158). Possible variations on the theme would be to keep the white and green elements and use orange blooms (chrysanthemums, marigolds, sunflowers) or flowers in shades of lilac and violet (pansies, lilac, hydrangeas) as the contrast colours. Alternatively, this could be an absolute riot of flowers if you used up lots of different fabrics scattered all over the quilt, with a simple contrast fabric (e.g. a spot) to prevent it from going too rampantly wild.

The fifth fabric is the white-on-green dotty fabric, which not only acts as a foil and background, but it also suggests the layers of net petticoats that often lay beneath the full skirts. This is 'Apple Pie' by American Jane Patterns, designed by Sandy Klop for Moda. And, as I had bought quite a few metres of it in a sale, I felt I should honour the idea of make-do-and-mend dressmaking and use it for the back as well.

For the binding, I used a lovely emerald green and small white polka dot fabric made by the Japanese company, Lecien (which markets a fantastic range of quilters' 'basics' such as dots and stripes), to give a definite but complementary frame to a quilt.

Note: The following designers create beautiful floral fabrics that would be suitable for this style of quilt: Kaffe Fassett, Philip Jacobs, Anna Maria Horner, Heather Bailey, Martha Negley, Jennifer Paganelli.

design

I came up with this design after a long time of wondering how I could suggest the gathering in of fabrics in dresses and the way they fall in folds so that you don't see all of the pattern at once; also how to hint at the way skirts swish, swirl and move as the wearer walks. Yet it had to be very simple and effective and show off plenty of the gorgeous fabric detail.

So I came up with a basic but very flexible series of rows that can be extended or increased depending on the size of quilt you want to make. Each row features two floral fabrics plus the contrasting spot, and I have repeated the pattern over the quilt. So rows 1, 3 and 5 have fabrics A and B, while rows 2 and 4 have fabrics C and D.

Each row is 16in (40.5cm) deep (finished measurement), but the strips within them vary in width and all the fabrics were cut separately and randomly; they measure from 1½–5in (4–12.5cm) (finished width). You may feel nervous cutting randomly, but I assure you that it is very easy and very liberating. Just don't go too thin or far too wide, or the quilt will look unbalanced.

✂ materials

Fabric suggestions: This quilt is the exception to my usual rule of not buying all the fabrics in one go and/ or from a single collection. It makes it a good project for beginners or for quilters who do not have a large collection of fabrics to hand, as fabrics can be bought in one shopping trip and/ or from a single designer or collection.

- - - - - - - - - - - - - - - - - - - -

Quilt top: It requires 1 yd/ m each of four floral fabrics plus 1½yd/ m of a contrasting fabric (in this case, the spotty fabric). (There will be leftovers of the floral fabrics used on rows 2 and 4, but you need the full yard or metre.) Or use a larger number of floral fabrics from half-yard/ half-metre pieces and make the quilt as large or small as you like.

- - - - - - - - - - - - - - - - - - - -

Backing: You will need 5yd (4.5m) of backing fabric.

- - - - - - - - - - - - - - - - - - - -

Binding: You will need ½yd/ m of fabric to make the binding.

- - - - - - - - - - - - - - - - - - - -

You will also need:

- A piece of wadding 3–4in (7.5–10cm) larger all around than the quilt top (I use 100 per cent organic cotton with scrim).
- 100 per cent cotton all-purpose sewing thread in ecru or taupe for the machine piecing.
- 100 per cent cotton quilting thread.

- - - - - - - - - - - - - - - - - - - -

Finished measurements: 62 x 80in (157.5 x 203cm).

The quilt has five rows made up of random-width strips.

✎ directions

All seam allowances are ¼in (6mm) unless otherwise stated.

— Whittle down the fabric selection by playing with fabrics folded into thin strips. I started by checking the suitability of each fabric by cutting out two to three strips of each of the possibles and playing with these first before committing all my lovely fabric.

— Cut out the strips. They should be 16½in (42cm) long and vary from 2–5½in (5–14cm) wide. I cut out every strip separately, as I wanted to get a good/ interesting part of a pattern into each strip. You do not need to cut out all the fabrics before starting to lay them out.

— Now lay out the strips in a row approx. 65in (165cm) long (you can make the quilt bigger if preferred, but do make allowances with the wadding, plus extra backing and binding fabric). There is no repeat pattern in my version (although there is nothing to stop you creating one), and the whole thing was laid out quickly and spontaneously. Sometimes I put floral strips next to each other and sometimes I keep them separate, with spots on either side.

— Build up the five rows (or more if you are making a bigger quilt). Don't worry too much at this point about them all being exactly the same width, but try to get the edges as close as possible.

— Now pick up the rows of strips so that you make a pile of strips, moving from left to right. Number them with Post-It notes or paper scraps pinned to the piles so you know the order in which to piece them together.

— Machine-piece the rows, one at a time, with a ¼in (6mm) seam allowance. Make sure you alternate the direction of the seam-sewing with each strip, working from top to bottom, then bottom to top and so on, so that the rows remain rectangular.

— Now iron each row, pressing the seams to face first in one direction and then in the opposite direction on the row below, alternating direction with each row.

— Lay out the flat, ironed horizontal rows in the correct order (keep the numbers pinned to the rows until you have sewn the whole quilt top) and check the widths. Add a strip or two where necessary to make all rows exactly the same width. Press the extra seams.

— Sew the five rows together to make the quilt top and press the horizontal seams in the same direction each time, and then iron the top of the quilt.

— Make the back by sewing two widths of backing fabric of equal length (I would allow 90in/228.5cm) together, with a ½in (1cm) seam allowance. (Trim the selvedges first if preferred.) Press this seam open and iron the whole back so that it is smooth and crease-free. The back should be 3–4in (7.5–10cm) larger than the quilt top.

— Now make the quilt sandwich and pin. (See page 142 for more information.)

— I chose to hand-quilt in vertical lines, so that the eye follows the horizontal 'folds' and 'pleats' of the design. I sewed straight lines along the entire length of the quilt, which sometimes follow seams and sometimes fall in the middle of a strip. Use masking tape as a line-guide where necessary. My lines are between 2½–5in (6–12.5cm) apart and I used emerald green Mettler 100 per cent cotton quilting thread. Trim the quilt sandwich so that the edges of the top, bottom and wadding are all the same.

— Make the binding and attach to the quilt (see page 143 for further information).

— Now wish for glorious summers and an abundance of pretty floral frocks.

More floral frock inspiration:

Floral Frocks by Rosemary Harden and Jo Turney (Antique Collectors' Club, 2007).

Vintage dress patterns and magazines.

Contemporary floral summer dresses inspired by the success of, and interest in, the exhibition.

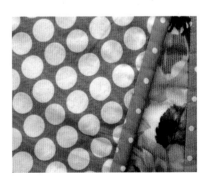

postage
stamp

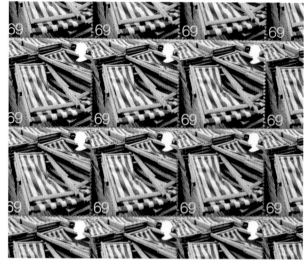

I admit it: I enjoy the occasional flirtation with philately. I'm not exactly a stamp collector, but I find beautiful stamps make postal correspondence much more enjoyable. When I was little, I made albums of stamps but always wanted to collect the prettiest and the most colourful, not the rarest and most valuable, and these days I'm not above asking for 'interesting' stamps when I buy, rather than simply taking what I'm offered, because those Post Office drawers and books often contain exceptionally lovely stamps.

A good stamp is a miniature work of art. In fact, I've been framing some of the most interesting and intriguing British stamps for years. We have tiny illustrations of trains and pantomimes, autumn fruits and storybook characters on our walls, and they never fail to catch my eye as I walk past.

But I also like the classic, definitive, Machin series British stamp, the one with the Queen's head in profile; the simple, etched design that comes in a huge range of values and colours. I wouldn't necessarily choose to buy these stamps all the time, as a single colour doesn't look that special on an envelope, but when you start to mix and match, it does get interesting. There are so many shades and hues that I could happily create a whole patchwork of different-value stamps on envelopes. All this is what set me thinking about a 'stamp' quilt in some of the lovely, pure, painterly colours used by the Royal Mail – colours with names straight out of the paintbox: raw sienna, burnt sienna, yellow ochre, raw umber, burnt umber, cobalt blue, Prussian blue, indigo blue and silver.

At is happens, I also very much like the two- or three-colour quilting fabrics that contain etched designs (usually flowers and foliage). With their wonderful colours and small-scale patterns, they closely resemble the Machin stamp style. I've been collecting them in a similar fashion to the way I collect stamps – as and when I find something that really pleases me. So when I thought about a stamp quilt, I knew I had a few fabrics to get me started, fabrics that I'd had difficulty using elsewhere because of their palette and scale.

design

As for the design, I had a ready-made source of inspiration. 'Stamp' quilts or 'postage stamp' quilts have been around for a long time. Traditionally, they are made with tiny squares set in regular arrangements or a structured pattern. Another version of this type of scrap quilt is the 'Trip Around the World', a name that nicely sums up the possibilities a stamp offers to a letter or card. This, too, is made with a huge number of fabrics cut into tiny squares (as small as 1in/ 2.5cm or 1½in/ 4cm), which are set in a regular pattern in which the lines of squares (either placed as straight-edge squares or 'on point', as square diamonds) radiate further and further out from the centre as the quilt progresses. I see this as a sort of 'home, sweet home' design, with the centre square as home, the place from which all trips and journeys begin.

When it came to square size, though, I knew my limits. Much as I admire the traditional stamp quilts made with small scraps, I have to admit that I draw the line at dealing with 1in (2.5cm) squares, so I decided

that 2in (5cm) squares (finished size) would be much easier to handle but would still create the desired effect of small 'stamps'. In fact, putting this quilt together is a little like building up a stamp album: it is quite painstaking and methodical, and requires fine motor skills plus the ability to suppress sneezes that might blow all the carefully laid-out pieces out of place.

There is a much quicker way of making this type of quilt, though, which avoids the method of laying everything out square by square. Many people use a strip method, whereby you sew together long strips of fabric (here they would be 2½in/ 6cm wide, so that the finished squares are 2in/ 5cm), and then cut across the sewn-together pieces to produce strips of squares. Now, this is fine if you are happy to take the risk that the fabrics will work well next to each other, but there is a good chance that one or two might not. So I made mine in a more time-consuming manner (it took me all of an afternoon to set out this quilt), and cut out all my squares and then placed each individual square where it belonged. By doing it this way, I found I could rectify mistakes and clashes easily. And there certainly were a few of those.

I started off working from the centre square and built up the pattern by working outwards from this point. Initially, I set the squares on their straight edges but soon saw that the effect of having them on their points, as square diamonds, was much more interesting and visually exciting. I then changed my work position so that I could view the layout differently to see diamonds rather than squares. And when did I decide to stop? Simple: when I ran out of fabric. I know that skilled quilters can make clever substitutions when they run out of a specific fabric, but my objective was to achieve a

specific effect, not to make a larger quilt. There is also something very liberating about simply setting out to make a pleasing quilt, rather than one of a certain size. It allows you to work with and make the most of what you've got, and it gives you permission to stop when you are satisfied.

♀ fabrics

Choosing the fabrics was a real pleasure once I had my source of inspiration. I already had a few two- and three-colour fabrics in pure, painterly colours which fitted into a calm but definite palette that reflects the Machin stamp colours, and found that by sorting through my fabrics I could make an unusual variation on a yellow and blue quilt. Some of the fabrics were leftovers (some in very small quantities, but that doesn't matter for this type of quilt as it can be a great using-up exercise) and some were still untouched half-yards and half-metres, plus I bought one or two more fabrics such as the delightful 'Chestnut' print by Joel Dewberry to extend the range. But really, this is a 'stash' quilt, the modern-day version of a scrap quilt, one which uses up what you already have. If you have only a small piece of a lovely fabric that you want to use, place it close to the centre, where you won't need too many squares from it. If you have a larger length of a favourite design, it can be used once or twice and further from the centre.

I collected around twenty fabrics and used sixteen of them. They are all two- or three-colour fabrics, and all but two have small designs. I used two versions of Kaffe Fassett's 'Stencil Carnation' plus his 'Fruit Basket', a small grey seedling design from Denyse Schmidt's Flea Market Fancy collection, three fabulous Japanese prints from Purl Soho (no longer available, but Purl always has a stock of interesting and lovely Japanese fabrics) including a teacup print from the Yuwa Live Life collection and a cream flowers on blue print from the Yuwa Coccinelle collection. The toile is 'More Romance' by Alex Anderson for P&B Textiles, and the ochre fabric is a Jinny Beyer Palette fabric from RJR Fabrics. The spots are 'New York Retro' by Sharon Yenter for In The Beginning Fabrics, and Michael Miller's 'Dumb Dot'.

I decided against a border, even though this would have made the quilt larger (at 66 x 66in/ 167.5 x 167.5cm, it is not huge). This is because I wanted the 'stamps' to be the focus and to let the eye move all over the quilt, right up to the edges, and follow all the various lines. Also, the grey triangles make an effective edge and I felt no more was needed to enhance the look of the quilt. So I just added a simple binding in an inky colour, the kind of ink that is used in the old-fashioned fountain pens that writers of handwritten and hand-stamped letters might choose.

The decision about the backing fabric was simple: I used a small black dot on plain white fabric to suggest perforations in sheets of stamps. Whimsical, but true.

✎ materials

Fabric suggestions: It's possible to use a different fabric for each round (in this case, you would need twenty-four fabrics plus a fabric for the outer-edge triangles), but I chose to use a few fabrics more than once even though I did not have a set repeat pattern. Or you could use fewer fabrics and create a pattern through repeats (e.g. two, four or six fabrics repeated throughout). This quilt allows you to use up unexciting fabrics that look better in small areas – as long as you team them with splashes of colour (I used gold, sky blue, sapphire blue and white to lighten and brighten).

- - - - - - - - - - - - - - - - - -

Quilt top: You need a total of 5½yd/ m of fabric for the squares, in as many fabrics as you want to include. It is impossible to give an exact quantity for each individual fabric, as it depends on where in the quilt it is placed. So here are guidelines:

➤ If you are going to make a 'random' quilt similar to mine, the maximum you will need of any one fabric is ½yd/ m. If a fabric appears more than twice in a large round, then you will need more than ½yd/ m of it.

➤ I suggest you collect a mix of ½yd/ m, ⅓yd/ m and ¼yd/ m pieces.

➤ You can also use up small scraps of fabric close to the centre where only a few squares are needed.

Note: You will also need ½yd/ m of the fabric to make the outer-edge triangles (which can be one of the fabrics used as 'stamps').

- - - - - - - - - - - - - - - - - -

Backing: You will need 4¼yd (3.8m) of fabric for the backing.

- - - - - - - - - - - - - - - - - -

Binding: You will need 17½in (44.5cm) of fabric for the binding.

- - - - - - - - - - - - - - - - - -

Note: This quilt uses a lot more cotton sewing thread than the average quilt, so make sure you have plenty of 100 per cent cotton all-purpose sewing thread in neutral ecru or taupe by your sewing machine. Count on at least four reels for a quilt top this size.

- - - - - - - - - - - - - - - - - -

You will also need:

➤ A piece of wadding 70 x 70in (178 x 178cm) or 4in (10cm) larger all around than the quilt top (I use 100 per cent organic cotton with scrim).
➤ 100 per cent cotton quilting thread

- - - - - - - - - - - - - - - - - -

Finished measurements: 66 x 66in (167.5 x 167.5cm).

Putting the quilt together

Join strip 1 first, then the corner triangle (2), then strips 3, 4 and so on.

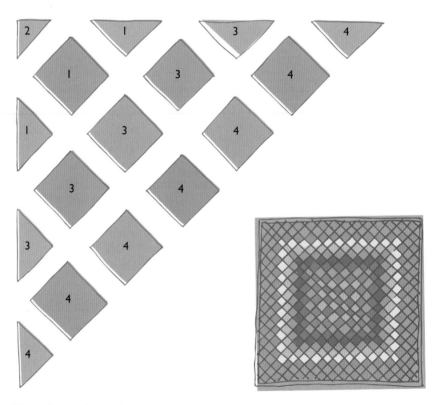

The quilt is made up of squares 'on point'. There are twenty-four across, and twenty-four down. There are twenty-three triangles around each outside edge, and a smaller triangle at each corner. See also the Hydrangea quilt on page 48.

directions

Notes

The number of squares increases with each round, so you will need one, four, eight, twelve, sixteen, twenty and so on, in increases of four, until you get to the twenty-fourth round – which requires ninety-two squares. However, I do not cut out in such a precise, mathematical manner as I never know which fabrics will go where until I start playing with them. So I suggest that you cut just a few squares from a handful of fabrics and begin by playing with these. Start at the centre, putting every square 'on point' so that it looks like a square diamond. Rearrange the squares if you are not happy, and cut and add more fabrics as the quilt grows. Do not be afraid to reject fabrics that do not fit in. The key is to make each fabric work well with its neighbour. I originally thought the rounds should melt into each other, but this made it look as though paints had run or my eyesight was going blurry. The quilt looked infinitely better when each fabric 'sang' out next to its neighbour as a definite statement/ contrast. In this way, each square of squares became a frame for the next line.

— All seam allowances are $\frac{1}{4}$in (6mm) unless otherwise stated.

— All squares should be cut to 2½in (6cm) so that they will be 2in (5cm) finished size.

— For a quilt this size, with twenty-four rounds, you need to cut ninety-two triangles for the outside edge. Make these by cutting out forty-six 2⅞in (7cm) squares, then cut these diagonally into two triangles each. To make the small corner triangles, cut one 3¼in (8cm) square into four triangles.

— Once you have laid out the quilt and are happy with it, pick it up row by row, starting at the top left-hand corner, and sew the squares together to make diagonal rows. See the diagram for the 'side-on' order in which to pick up and piece this quilt.

— Each time you have machine-pieced a diagonal strip, remember to reattach the number sticker so that you know the order in which to sew the strips together.

— Dealing with triangles can be tricky at first, until you have got used to it. I unpicked quite a few triangles sewn to a square, because I found that the angles didn't meet in the right places, or I had pieced them the wrong way up. But with practice, you will soon learn to see how to join the two pieces of fabric together. Just take your time, don't rush and don't panic. The worst that can happen is that you'll have to unpick it and try again.

— Iron all the individual strips, pressing the seams on odd-numbered rows one way and the other way on even-numbered rows, so that the seams sit neatly on the back. Iron both sides.

— Now build up the quilt top by sewing the strips together in the correct sequence. Do not start the seam of each strip from the same end, as the quilt may end up more as a parallelogram than a square. I place a pin at the end of the strip I'm currently sewing to mark where I should start the next line of sewing.

— Iron the top again, first on the back, pressing all the seams in one direction, then on top.

— Make the back by sewing two widths, 74in (188cm) long, together with a central ½in (1cm) seam. The back should be 3–4in (7.5–10cm) larger all around than the quilt top. Press the seam open. You will trim the excess fabric at the sides when you make the quilt sandwich.

— Make the quilt sandwich (see page 142 for instructions).

— The quilt is now ready to be quilted. I used simple rows of small running stitches that were in keeping with the scale of the squares. I wanted to bring out the vertical and horizontal lines that go through the squares, so stitched straight lines through every other square in a grid using a Mettler quilting thread in a deep indigo.

— Trim the edges with scissors (or a rotary cutter if you want a very straight edge) and make and attach the binding (see page 143 for further instructions).

— Go off on a trip around the world.

purple
rain

I don't own any vintage quilts, although I sometimes think it must be lovely to have a collection not only to use and admire, but also to provide valuable inspiration. Instead, I make do with looking at vintage quilts in books, visits to friends' houses where I can see beautiful old quilts still gracing beds and furniture, and the occasional trip to a quilt fair or exhibition where, if I am lucky, there will be someone showing old quilts. Once I was very lucky, and saw some quilts from Kaffe Fassett's personal collection; one quilt in particular stayed with me, and it is this that inspired the Purple Rain quilt.

I saw it at the 'Festival of Quilts', having already fallen in love with it in Kaffe's book, *Passionate Patchwork* (see page 152). It's a Half Log Cabin design in which the blocks are built up around a square but only on two sides, instead of four as in the full Log Cabin. Kaffe's quilt uses dozens of different cotton fabrics in mostly primary colours, and probably dates from the 1930s. I liked this vintage look so much that I tried to create something similar, but as I didn't (and still don't) have enough fabrics and scraps in the correct palette, my first attempt turned out to be a visual mess.

I was disappointed, but still determined to use this wonderful design – which looks complex but is in fact very straightforward to sew. And then one day, as I was thinking about it during a long car journey, it suddenly occurred to me that it would work as a colour story, exploiting many different variations on a favourite colour. And that unifying colour would be purple, because I had a growing pile of purple-themed fabrics with lots of lilacs, violets, mauves, plums, lavenders, periwinkles, aubergines and heliotropes.

Although I'd thought of it as purple during the making, and even called the quilt the 'Purple Rain' quilt because of the scattering of flecks of purple (and because I found myself singing the song by Prince as I sewed and quilted), it is really more of a meditation on lilac, because the darker purple fabrics did

not work in the quilt as well as I'd imagined. Despite the presence of contrasting colour detail (from bright yellow to viridian, turquoise to deep pink), the overarching theme is lilac, and the quilt has turned out to be a real celebration of a favourite colour in an old-fashioned patchwork style and a fresh, pretty effect. (A blue or yellow theme could also work beautifully.)

I was also inspired by the deep lilac toile fabric designed by Jennifer Paganelli for the Sis Boom Mod Girls collection and had been determined to get it into a quilt, even though initially I could not imagine how I could put such a formal design into a quilt without it, too, becoming too formal. Then I saw that it would work perfectly with other lilacs and purples, and that the formality could be offset both by the Half Log Cabin design and by the use of the marvellously lush 'Lilac Rose' pattern by Philip Jacobs on the back, binding and in the quilt top.

design

The design is a Half Log Cabin, which is built up by adding strips to two sides of a square (it has also been used to great effect by the quilters of Gee's Bend), and I wanted to use this traditional design without any significant alteration. The only changes I made were to the measurements; the strips in the original quilt were something like 1⅛in (28mm) wide, but I could not face cutting strips to the nearest eighth of an inch, so decided instead to have strips 1in (2.5cm) wide (finished width) and 4in (10cm) squares (finished size). But I did want to recreate the same ratio of strips to squares, so kept five strips in each block, so that each finished block measures 9 x 9in (23 x 23cm).

I did not have a master plan for the quilt size, but decided to stop making the Half Log Cabin blocks when I had six across and seven down. If I'd had all the time in the world, I would have carried on until the quilt reached double-bed proportions (I imagined sitting up in bed with a cup of tea looking at all those lovely patterns and combinations), but I had to be realistic.

This quilt is, admittedly, quite time-consuming to make. However, I found that I could piece a block in fifteen minutes once I'd got into the rhythm of sewing. So if you want to make a six-block by eight-block quilt, it would take a total of just twelve hours to put together the blocks, which could be a very enjoyable project to sew over the course of a week or weekend. Add in a couple of hours for cutting out the squares and strips, approximately five hours to sew up the blocks and the borders, time to make the backing and then the quilt sandwich, plus a few nights of hand-quilting, and you can have this quilt made in anything from one to three weeks (less if you do it non-stop). The result makes the time commitment very worthwhile.

To extend my quilt, I decided to add a border (the original quilt did not have a border – or a back). I used a narrow 2in (5cm) border in a thin, floral spotty fabric ('Sweet Dew' from Kei Fabric) to create a frame around the quilt and to contrast with the wider 5in (12.5cm) outer border in the toile design (the toile fabric would not have stood out sufficiently from the body of the quilt without the thinner spotty border). For the top and bottom borders, I cut the toile fabric widthways in order to get the scene going across, and for the side borders I cut it lengthways to get the scene going down the sides.

fabrics

The key to this sort of quilt is to plan the look of the quilt before you get going. So decide on a mood or colour, make piles of fabric, and add and subtract over and over again until you have a good selection of fabrics that work extremely well and closely together. My initial idea was to make a quilt with a simple purple story, and then I realized that it was gravitating towards a lilac with purple/ mauve/ violet and even viridian highlights, and that the key to the look was freshness – I took out anything that was dull and/ or muted, even though it could be called lilac or mauve. Once I had sorted out the look, I could tell quickly what did and didn't work.

Try to include a wide variety of fabrics, because this quilt looks best with a thrifty vintage look. To test fabrics, I unfolded and bunched up various designs on the floor and took out the ones that didn't work by dint of scale, tone, shade or pattern. I decided to keep the white-on-purple polka dots in strips (but not in the squares); even though it could be seen as too dominant, it breaks up lines and helps the eye to move around the quilt.

For the squares I used the fabrics with bigger, bolder patterns that could be framed by the other fabrics (having said that, some of the large-scale fabrics – particularly those by Philip Jacobs – looked excellent in thin strips). I used eight fabrics for the squares and eighteen or so fabrics for the strips. Depending on how much fabric I started with, some appear only once or twice, and some appear all over the top.

The fabrics in my quilt include a large vegetable print, a purple scattered chrysanthemums print and a deep purple coneflower print, all by Martha Negley; Lilac 'Stencil Flower', Lilac 'Spots', Lavender 'Minton' and Mauve 'Guinea Flower', all by Kaffe Fassett; 'Sweet Dew' from Kei Fabric (also in the narrow border); the Sis Boom/Jennifer Paganelli toile (also in the wide border); a leftover pansy print; two Amy Butler fabrics from the Temple Flowers collection; plus three colourways of Philip Jacobs's 'Lilac Rose' (Pink, Taupe and Mint – the latter is also the backing and binding fabric), and his Pink 'Luscious', Taupe 'Blowsey' and Lavender 'Ivy'. (Philip's huge floral designs cut up incredibly well, with plenty of lovely surprises.) This mix gives a bright, cheerful and full-of-spring freshness with suggestions of drifts of naturalized purple crocuses and a few egg yolk yellow and dark purple specimens thrown in.

The backing fabric is Mint 'Lilac Rose' by Philip Jacobs, a design I would love to have as curtains, so a large expanse of it on the back of a quilt is the next best thing. I could perhaps have chosen something small and sprigged, but I saw this as an opportunity to use a fabric I adore. And why not? Why keep a gorgeous fabric in a cupboard when you can have it in a quilt where you can admire it all the time? I also used this fabric for the binding, because I simply didn't have enough of anything else in the pile and there were enough leftovers from trimming the back.

materials

Fabric suggestions: It's good if you can treat this as a scrap quilt as far as possible. Gather all your offcuts and see if there is a colour story you can create with them, or if it's possible to make a multicoloured version (e.g. primary colours, 1930s reproduction fabrics). Alternatively, be guided by a favourite fabric (I was inspired by the Jennifer Paganelli lilac toile fabric) and collect fabrics to work with it. Apart from the toile fabric, I did not buy anything specifically for this quilt top.

- - - - - - - - - - - - - - - - - -

Quilt top: To make the Half Log Cabin, you will need 5yd (4.5m) of fabric. You will need a maximum of ½yd/ m of any one fabric. Allow for eighteen to twenty fabrics, in scraps and pieces from 5–18in (12.5–45.5cm), so that you can make an interestingly varied top.

Alternatively, the Half Log Cabin blocks could be made entirely from scraps and leftovers.

- - - - - - - - - - - - - - - - - -

The blocks are
a Half Log Cabin design.

The quilt has six blocks across and eight blocks down, plus a border.

Borders: You need ½yd/ m of fabric for a 2in (5cm) border and 1yd/ m for a 5in (12.5cm) outer border.

- - - - - - - - - - - - - - - - - -

Backing: You will need 5yd (4.5m) of fabric for the backing and this will also give enough leftovers to make the binding. The quantities also allow for large pattern repeats.

- - - - - - - - - - - - - - - - - -

Binding: If you choose to use a different fabric for the binding, you will need ½yd/ m fabric.

- - - - - - - - - - - - - - - - - -

You will also need:

- A piece of wadding 3–4in (7.5–10cm) larger all around than the quilt top (I use 100 per cent organic cotton with scrim).
- 100 per cent cotton all-purpose sewing thread in ecru or taupe for the machine piecing.
- 100 per cent cotton quilting thread.

- - - - - - - - - - - - - - - - - -

Final measurements: 66in wide x 75½in long (167.5 x 192cm).

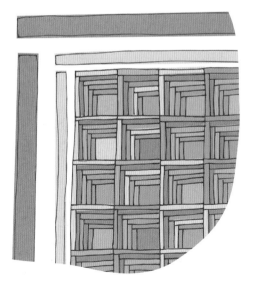

directions

All seam allowances are ¼in (6mm) unless otherwise stated.

— Making a Half Log Cabin (or Log Cabin) quilt is one of the very few times I work block by block, and not by creating a full layout before sewing. (It is not possible to make the layout in advance because the strips are not pre-cut.)

— The blocks can be made on a production line basis, i.e. adding first strips to all blocks, then second strips to all blocks and so on. I started this way, but then realized that I wanted to have a good variety of inner squares and for each block to have its own style, so decided to create each one individually.

— There is a huge number of possible combinations with this number of fabrics. I tried moving from lighter to darker fabrics, and vice versa, as I worked out from the square, but then found that deliberately muddling up the fabrics and a mix of planned and spontaneous sequences gives the right measure of vibrancy and interest.

— Start by cutting out a number of 4½in (11cm) squares (you will need a total of forty-two for this size of quilt, but you can cut out more as you go along and see what is working well). Select eight to ten fabrics with interesting/ bigger/ bolder designs for the squares and fussy-cut if necessary so that you get the best parts of the design in them – the details your eye will pick out amongst the density of pattern elsewhere.

— Then cut out a few strips, 1½in (4cm) wide, from each of your fabrics (as long as possible, preferably selvedge to selvedge – you will trim as you go along). Keep the squares and strips by the sewing machine. Cut more 4½in (11cm) squares and 1½in (4cm) strips as you go along.

— Choose a square and five fabrics to go around it, and build up the blocks in the traditional Log Cabin style, but only on two sides (left and top) of the square. Note that it is very important to change the direction of sewing for each border strip, otherwise the block will become a parallelogram, not a square. Always start with the left-hand strip and sew from bottom to top, then add the upper strip and sew from right to left. Trim the end of the strip after sewing with scissors or rotary cutter, and return reusable strips to the pile.

— Iron each block after making, pressing all seams in the same direction. Ironing is crucial: clever ironing can bring a wonky square back into shape. Keep the iron nearby for convenience.

— Once you have made all the blocks, lay them out to your preferred pattern. Arrange them so that there are not too many of the same fabrics near each other.

— Pick up the rows or columns and put into piles with clear markers on, so you know which row is which.

— Sew the blocks together to create rows, remembering to start each subsequent line of stitching at the end where you left off. Press the seams in alternating directions for each row.

— Then sew the rows together to make the top and iron, pressing the seams in the same direction.

— Make the border by cutting out strips and sewing them together. Attach the side borders first, and then the top and bottom borders. Press the seams towards the outer edge.

— Make the backing by sewing two widths of fabric together with a ½in (1cm) seam (trim the selvedges first, if preferred). The backing should be 3–4in (7.5–10cm) larger all around than the top. Iron and press the seam open.

— Make the quilt sandwich (see page 142 for further instructions) and trim the excess backing fabric and wadding to 2in (5cm) all round.

— Hand-quilt following seam lines or using masking tape to mark the lines of stitching. I used a purple thread and stitched diagonal lines of running stitches across the quilt.

— Trim the edges of the quilt with scissors or a rotary cutter.

— Make and attach the binding (see page 143 for further instructions).

— Sit and marvel at the ingenuity of traditional quilt patterns and the beauty and detail of quilt fabrics.

More vintage and traditional quilt inspiration:

American Quilt Classics by Patricia Cox (Collins & Brown, 2001).

Country Quilts by Linda Seward (Mitchell Beazley, 1996).

The Quilters' Guild Collection (David & Charles, 2005).

The Quilts of Gee's Bend by John Beardsley (Tinwood Books, 2002).

Kaffe Fassett's V&A Quilts by Kaffe Fassett with Liza Prior Lucy (Ebury Press, 2005).

hammock

You simply cannot beat a good stripe for quilt inspiration, and I am especially inspired by the classic stripes of the woven canvases used to make deckchairs and hammocks. Whether it's the traditional deckchair stripe in red, blue or green and white, or the more colourful Indian or Caribbean-style stripe that you see on hammocks, sun loungers, windbreaks, swinging chairs and awnings, they all speak of summer and lazing in the garden, reading, dozing, rocking and swaying, gazing at the sky and enjoying a warm breeze. They make you think of good books and refreshing drinks, the sounds of the garden, and peacefulness. And this stripy quilt is not only inspired by the stripes of hammocks and deckchairs, it is also suitable for use on them.

I was also inspired by the amazing 'Delphinium' design by Philip Jacobs and wanted to make a quilt to show off this fabric. I was drawn to it because it reminded me of the fantastic 1920s and 1930s wallpapers I'd seen in the 'Flights of Fancy' exhibition at the Whitworth Art Gallery in Manchester. This featured decorative wallpaper friezes, cut-out panels, and borders in wild cottage garden flower designs including a very tastefully over-the-top 'Delphinium Decoration' with life-size flowers up to an adult's shoulder. (It also echoed the flower-filled, hand-embroidered textiles and the crinoline lady and cottage garden designs of the period that I like so much.)

I hadn't seen the fabric in real life before I ordered it from Glorious Color (www.gloriouscolor.com) and I had a wonderful surprise when I opened the package and unfolded the lengths of fabric with their long, clever, vertical repeats and beautiful colours; I could happily have made a quilt from each of the fabric's six palettes, but restricted myself to two. The Pastel and the Slate colourways inspired me to make two very different Hammock quilt variations: one for summer days and one for summer evenings. With its pure, fresh colours, the Pastel fabric (not really pastel at all – it's much brighter) makes me think of English

gardens in June, pale blue skies and walking down a garden path with tall spires of deep blue delphiniums on either side. The Slate fabric makes me think of summer evenings, a garden in the gloaming, and the lazy pleasure of rocking in a hammock with a glass of Pimm's, smelling the scents and watching the light and colours change and fade.

No wonder I like stripes.

design

When I saw the way the fabric design and repeats worked over the two-yard piece I had bought, I knew I wouldn't be able to cut it up widthways and that I'd have to use it in lengths. So I cast around in my mind for suitable long stripe or column patterns that might work. I didn't know of any in quilt books I'd seen and, as the pastel colourway kept suggesting gorgeously fresh and fragrant summer days, the idea of a wide column bordered by a set of thinner stripes took hold, and all I then had to do was look at a few pictures of deckchairs and hammocks for further inspiration. I found plenty on Flickr (www.flickr.com) and on GAP Photos (www.gapphotos.com), but the best place for

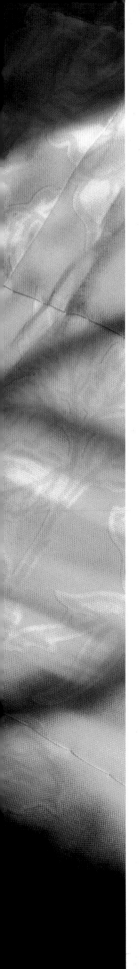

visual inspiration turned out to be Deckchair Stripes, a company that sells truly wonderful canvas and has a very colourful website (www.deckchairstripes.com).

I realized that there are so many variations on the hammock and deckchair stripe that I would never run out of ideas. There are regular stripes, random stripes, thick and thin stripes and combinations of the two, simple stripes and complex stripes. There can be two, three or four colours, or as many colours as you like. And this is the beauty of this quilt: simply transfer your own taste on to it and make something that pleases you and works with the fabric you own. It's very flexible – once you have the columns of your main fabric, it's entirely up to you what you put in between. I decided on four thin stripes, sewn together to make a wider section, which contrasts with the delphiniums, but it's possible to vary the thickness of the stripes and set them in different combinations, e.g. thin, thin, thick, thick or thin, thick, thin, thick or (as I have done in the Summer Day version) thin, thick, thick, thin.

The design is intended to be very simple and to inspire experiments with fabric. The essence of the quilt is to choose a main 'lead' fabric you love deeply and set it off with a simpler 'chorus' of fabrics that each pick out a colour or note to create something that really sings and dances.

As for the size, I was governed by the initial purchase of two yards of the main fabric, so this quilt became a single-bed/ one-person hammock size. You could lengthen it by buying 2¼yd/ m or 2½yd/ m and adjusting the thin stripes accordingly. I did not add a border, as hammocks and deckchairs do not have one, and also I was happy with the stripes just as they are.

fabrics

Summer Day version

I found the Summer Day quilt very easy to put together. All I had to do was take my cue from the lovely colours already there in the 'Delphinium' fabric. I wanted to keep to fresh colours with whites and/ or small patterns, so that the delphiniums would still stand out. I matched the colours carefully and they had to be just the right shade. But even when they were the right shade, they didn't all automatically work; I rejected a deep sapphire blue and a rich coral pink because even though these colours appear in the main fabric, they were too dark for the look and feel of the quilt. In the end I selected a generic pretty pink spot, a large white spot on pale duck-egg blue (with no selvedge so no company information), Lime 'Aboriginal Dot' by Kaffe Fassett and the lilac/ lavender version of 'Karen' from the Girlfriends collection by Jennifer Paganelli/ Sis Boom. The finished widths of the stripes in order of placement are pink spot 1in (2.5cm), lilac scroll 2in (5cm), blue spot 2in (5cm), lime spot 1in (2.5cm).

For the back, I knew I wanted something fresh and clean and had thought of using blue (to evoke the blue skies seen from hammocks and deckchairs), but when I came across 'Pop Garden' in Lime by Heather Bailey, with its white rose outlined in the same duck-egg/ aqua blue that appears on the top, I found the perfect summer's day match.

Right: Summer Day version

Summer Evening version

I was so taken with the unusual palette of the Slate 'Delphinium' print that I also made a Summer Evening version, for real or imaginary relaxation in deckchairs and hammocks just as the light is failing and flowers are visible only as patches of colour, and the scents of roses and night-scented stock are at their sweetest. I picked out some of the lighter rather than darker colours, and used a white on pale blue spot, a tiny white spot on mid-green, the pink 'Stencil Carnation' by Kaffe Fassett and the green on white 'Coral' design by Philip Jacobs, which also appears as the binding. The finished widths of the stripes in order of placement are blue spot 1½in (4cm), 'Coral' 1in (2.5cm), green spot 1in (2.5cm), 'Stencil Carnation' 2½in (6cm).

For the backing I chose the strange and wonderful large-scale 'Begonia Leaves', also by Philip Jacobs, in an equally unusual palette that continues the silvery evening theme with the types of colours that are produced when the light fades and plays tricks with your eyes, and plants and flowers seem to glow.

Note: The following designers and companies produce large-scale fabrics that would work well in this quilt: Anna Maria Horner, Heather Bailey, Jennifer Paganelli, Tina Givens, Amy Butler, Kaffe Fassett, Philip Jacobs, Martha Negley, Ro Gregg for Northcott, Alexander Henry and Benartex.

Right: Summer Evening version

materials

Fabric suggestions: This quilt is a mixture of thrift/ using up what you have and splashing out on 2yd/ m of a gorgeous, large-scale fabric, but as there is an exact science to calculating the quantities of the fabrics, there should not be any leftovers and wastage.

Choose a big print that you really love and want to see in a quilt, or use something you've been unsure about cutting into, because you will be able to admire it in this design.

– – – – – – – – – – – – – – – – – –

Quilt top: You will need 2yd/ m of the main fabric to go in the wide stripes.

You will also need four fabrics to make the thinner stripes. You need to make four strips 2yd/ m long from each fabric, to go into each of the four-stripe sections between the main fabric. This section should be 6in (15cm) wide when finished, so you must decide on the combination of stripe widths before cutting out.

For a quilt this length, the following amounts of fabric will give you enough for four 2yd/ m stripes (I am giving finished width here): 1in (2.5cm) stripes use 12in (30cm) fabric; 1½in (4cm) stripes use 16in (40.5cm) fabric; 2in (5cm) stripes use 20in (51cm) fabric; 2½in (6cm) stripes use 24in (60cm) fabric.

– – – – – – – – – – – – – – – – – –

Backing: You will need 4½yd (4.1m) of fabric for the backing.

– – – – – – – – – – – – – – – – – –

Binding: You will need 17½in (44.5cm) of fabric for the binding.

– – – – – – – – – – – – – – – – – –

You will also need:

– A piece of wadding 3–4in (7.5–10cm) larger all around than the quilt top (I use 100 per cent organic cotton with scrim).
– 100 per cent cotton all-purpose sewing thread in ecru or taupe for the machine piecing.
– 100 per cent cotton quilting thread.

– – – – – – – – – – – – – – – – – –

Finished measurements: 60in wide x 69in long (152 x 175cm).

directions

All seam allowances are $\frac{1}{4}$in (6mm) unless otherwise stated.

– This is a five-star quilt when it comes to speed and simplicity, and it's possible to lay it out and machine-piece it in one day.

– Cut the main fabric into four equal strips lengthways. I cut mine into four 9½in (24cm) strips, but I could have got four 10in (25cm) strips out of the 42in (106cm) width. Make sure you label each strip 1–4, in the correct order, as you cut them from left to right, because you will want them to appear this way in the quilt.

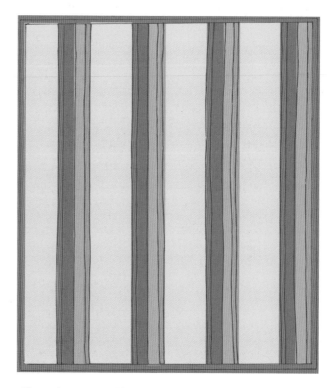

The quilt consists of four wide columns of a single fabric, plus four columns made up from four thin strips.

— Now cut out the strips to go in between the pieces of the main fabric, with a ¼in (6mm) seam allowance. These should make a total finished width of 6in (15cm) and can be in any combination of widths (see opposite in Materials section). Cut eight strips across the widths of each of the four striped fabrics to your chosen measurement.

— Trim the selvedges and make four strips by joining sets of two strips together with a ¼in (6mm) seam. If you find all the joining seams are likely to appear in the same place and thus create an unsightly line, you can move the seams by cutting a strip into two and sewing the shorter pieces to either end of the longer strip.

— Press the seams open.

— The strips will probably be different lengths at this point, but you will trim them after machine-piecing the quilt top.

— Make the inner striped sections by sewing together the four strips in the correct order, remembering to alternate the direction of sewing with each strip by beginning a new one at the end where you finished the previous one so that no distortion occurs. Try to keep the ends of the top edge as level and even as possible.

— Press the seams to one side, all in the same direction.

— Finish piecing the top by sewing the wide columns (A) to the striped sections (B) in an ABABABAB pattern. Try to keep the top edge as straight and even as possible.

— Press the seams to one side, all in the same direction.

— Trim the uneven ends with a ruler and rotary cutter so that top and bottom edges are straight.

— Make the backing by sewing together two widths of fabric, 77–78in (195.5–198cm) long, with a ½in (1cm) seam. Press the seam open and iron the back on both sides. You can trim any excess fabric when you make the quilt sandwich.

— Make the quilt sandwich (see page 142 for further instructions). Trim the wadding and backing so that they are 2in (5cm) larger than the top (unless you are having the quilting done professionally, in which case the excess should be 4in/ 10cm).

— Hand-quilt with 100 per cent quilting cotton. Create simple vertical lines with running stitch, using the seams as guidelines.

— Trim the edges using scissors or rotary cutter and ruler, so that they are all straight and equal.

— Make and attach the binding (see page 143 for further instructions).

— Take the quilt outside and swing in a real hammock or laze in a deckchair. Or think about doing so.

sample
book

Ever since my best friend Janet and I played with her mum's Avon Lady perfume and make-up sample boxes, I have always liked shade cards, paint charts, fabric swatches and testers. I also like the idea that, even if I can't have or own the whole of something lovely, I can at least see, touch, taste or smell a little sample of it.

When I discovered that the Cooper-Hewitt Museum was holding an exhibition of salesmen's sample books and shade cards at a time when I would be in New York, I had to see it. 'Multiple Choice; From Sample to Product' was small but beautifully formed, and featured the most exquisite books and cards of fabrics, paints, buttons, needles, wallpaper, lace and more. It was a treat to look at the choice and range, and to imagine the huge range of creative possibilities they suggested. I was entranced by the samples of products – often no more than small snippets of cotton fabrics or tiny samples of luminous enamels – all carefully cut out or painted, lined up and entered into a book or catalogue. The exhibition confirmed that sample books and shade cards have a fascinating beauty of their own.

It was this idea of tasters and testers arranged in a very practical, yet artful way, that inspired me to make a quilt. The result is simply a textile version of one of the many types of vintage fabric sample books, and it's fitting that there are many more possibilities because the sample card is all about choice, as the title of the exhibition suggests (I also fancy making quilts based on watercolour paint charts and yarn shade cards). My design is based on the sample books produced by A.B.C. Fabrics in America in the 1930s, with small triangles of fabric pasted on to the pages of a book. In fact, the exhibition made me think once again how every quilt is an exercise in multiple choice – something that can either be liberating or, at times, utterly overwhelming, especially today when we have vast numbers of fabrics available.

design

Have you ever walked into a fabric shop and wanted to buy every single colourway of a collection of fabrics simply because you love them all? Well, this quilt is designed to let you indulge in the pleasure of buying a small piece of a whole range to create a sample quilt of favourite fabrics.

Although I very much like the sample books that present fabrics in rectangles or strips, sometimes with fancy borders, I decided to use the A.B.C. cotton percale pages as inspiration (the website allowed me to view page after page of fabrics that had not faded because they had been so well preserved in a book), and to keep to the page layout as my design idea. So I used large rectangles made up of two triangles, one in a 'sample' fabric and one in a 'paper' fabric, although this design also lends itself to smaller rectangles if you prefer.

I laid out the quilt top before sewing and ended up with six rectangles across and ten down – it would have been very easy to make it larger, smaller, longer or wider by adding or taking away rectangles. I decided to use a random pattern with fabric 'samples' scattered about, but also think a quilt in which each design appears in a single row, like the samples in the books, would look good. (In fact, it might be a good idea to plan a quilt by gluing little triangles of fabric on to a page and working out optimum positions and arrangements this way.) I did find that some fabrics worked better than others; the dark blue colourways were particularly good because they gave definition in a relatively calm, plain quilt.

fabrics

To be in keeping with the inspiration behind this quilt, the fabrics needed to be retro, 'Aunt Grace' or 1930s reproduction designs – and there is no shortage of these on the market. As soon as I saw the full range of the Wee Play by American Jane Patterns collection, by Sandy Klop for Moda, I thought they would be ideal for this quilt – plus I liked the fresh, cheerful colours, and the way they all worked well together (something they are designed to do, of course). So I bought six colours each of two designs with a sunny, pretty, vintage feel that would not look out of place on summer dresses and aprons. They look as if they could have been printed on unbleached calico, which means they work with the four plain, cream-based fabrics that represent the paper of the book's pages. For these I chose fabrics with tiny patterns or woven stripes that look like ink pen marks, ruled lines or watermarks on paper. This is very deliberately a cooler, plainer and calmer theme than most of my other quilts.

The border is made from two blue fabrics from the top (I used two because I didn't have enough of any one fabric), and the binding is the yellow floral fabric that appears in the 'samples'. I wanted the backing fabric to resemble a sample book cover, and found a different fabric from the same collection which continues the theme but also contrasts with the flowery fabrics in the quilt top.

I added a border, even though the cotton percale sample book pages do not have one; I wanted it to be a kind of margin and used two of the dark blue fabrics (which make me think of scribbles and notes written in blue ink).

I then kept the hand quilting very simple, but made it deliberately noticeable by using a deep blue thread on the 'paper' triangles so that it appears like marks, notes and numbers written on the sample book pages.

materials

Fabric suggestions: This is an opportunity to use lots of lovely 1930s/ 'Aunt Grace'/ feedsack reproduction fabrics with small designs and sweet colours. For more ideas, see Variations opposite.

- - - - - - - - - - - - - - - - - - -

Quilt top: For the quilt top, excluding the border, you will need a total of 2½yd/ m plain fabrics and 2½yd/ m of patterned fabrics.

To make a 3½in (9cm) border (finished measurement), you will need 28in (71cm) of fabric.

- - - - - - - - - - - - - - - - - - -

Backing: You will need 5½yd (5m) of fabric to make the backing.

- - - - - - - - - - - - - - - - - - -

Binding: You will need 20in (51cm) of fabric to make the binding.

- - - - - - - - - - - - - - - - - - -

You will also need:

- A piece of wadding 3–4in (7.5–10cm) larger all around than the quilt top (I use 100 per cent organic cotton with scrim).
- 100 per cent cotton all-purpose sewing thread in ecru or taupe for the machine piecing.
- 100 per cent cotton quilting thread for machine or hand piecing.

- - - - - - - - - - - - - - - - - - -

Finished measurements: 69 x 87in (175 x 221cm).

directions

Notes

All seam allowances are ¼in (6mm) unless otherwise stated.

The blocks are made from long triangles cut from rectangles to make a finished block measuring 10½in (26.5cm) across and 8in (20cm) down. You can cut out the rectangles using a quilting ruler or a template made from thick cardboard, or the template plastic that is available from quilt shops and websites.

I found it useful to make a cardboard template of the rectangle and mark the TOP and BOTTOM triangles so that I could check before cutting that I was cutting along the correct line across the rectangle.

It is very easy to end up with the triangles facing the wrong way, and they are not reversible. For this, it is important to have all the fabrics facing the same way (i.e. right way up) if cutting in layers.

The quilt has six blocks across and ten down, so a total of sixty rectangles. In my quilt, the bottom triangle is always cream/ 'paper', and the upper triangle is always patterned/ 'sample', so you need to cut thirty cream/ paper rectangles to make sixty plain triangles and thirty patterned/ sample rectangles to make sixty patterned triangles. You may want to begin by cutting out a few trial blocks to see how they work, or you may be happy to cut out all the rectangles/ triangles in one go.

- The cut size of the made-up rectangles is 11 x 8½in (28 x 21.5cm), and the finished block will be 10½ x 8in (26.5 x 20cm). To make the rectangles, cut thirty 11½ x 8⅞in (29 x 22.5cm) rectangles of plain fabric, and the same number in patterned fabric. Cut each rectangle across diagonally into two long triangles (from top left corner to bottom right corner), cutting both plain and patterned fabrics in the same direction each time (see above before starting to cut).

- Make the rectangles by sewing together a top and bottom triangle. Iron each rectangle, pressing all the seams to one side. (I pressed the seams to the darker side so that the darker fabrics did not show up as a shadow on the paler fabrics. This also made it easier to hand-quilt, as the needle only had to go through the three layers of the quilt sandwich.)

The quilt is made up of blocks consisting of two long triangles. There are six blocks across and ten blocks down, plus a border.

— Trim the fabric at the corners to neaten the rectangles. Lay out the blocks to suit your taste or theme.

— Sew the rectangles together in rows. (Pick up each row of rectangles in the correct order and number each strip with a Post-It note so that you keep track of what goes where.) Iron each row, pressing the seams to one side, alternating direction with each row.

— Sew the strips of rectangles together to make the top. Iron, and press the seams towards the darker fabrics.

— Cut out the borders. Cut strips, 4in (10cm) wide, from full widths of fabric. Sew them together to make the border strips (sashing), pressing the seams open. Sew the borders to

the sides first and trim. Attach the borders to the top and bottom edges. Trim and iron.

— Make the backing. Using a ½in (1cm) seam allowance, sew together two widths of fabric, 95in (241cm) long. The backing needs to be 4in (10cm) larger all around than the quilt top.

— Make the quilt sandwich (see page 142). Trim the edges so that the backing and wadding are approx. 2in (5cm) larger than the quilt top.

— Machine- or hand-quilt. I hand-stitched lines of running stitch ¼in (6mm) in from the seams of the pale triangles, plus a line all around the border.

— Trim the quilt top so that all the edges are even.

— Make and attach the binding (see page 143 for further instructions).

— Put out the bunting, have a street party, or take a multiple choice test.

Variations:

The joy of this quilt is that there are all sorts of 'multiple choices' you can make with it.

— It is not essential to have plain 'paper' triangles: all the triangles could in fact be 'samples' of, say, a collection or a favourite designer or theme (e.g. flowers, American Civil War, 'Aunt Grace', reproduction feedsack fabrics).

— The quilt could be made in much brighter colours (or, indeed, in very pale pastels) for a different effect.

— It could be made with scrap fabrics and be called a 'bunting' quilt.

— I quilted this design at the seaside and saw that it could also be a nautical flag or semaphore quilt. It has a jaunty, seaside feel and this could be enhanced by using lots of blues and whites with pretty florals.

— Small-scale designs work well with a plainer 'paper' contrast, but a quilt that has rectangles made up of a large pattern in one triangle and a small pattern in the other would also work well.

— For further inspiration, visit the exhibition's website (http://www.cooperhewitt.org/exhibitions/multiple_choice/site/).

swimming
pool

My first impulse and basic inspiration was simply to make a blue quilt, a colour I felt I had not used a great deal. So I sorted through the few blue fabrics I owned, found that I was drawn to soft shades of aqua, bluebell, forget-me-not, duck egg and sky blue rather than variations on indigo or royal blue, then had a fine time building up a collection of interesting blue fabrics to go in my quilt over the course of a year or so.

Initially, I thought these would make a lovely snowball quilt (one in which the four corners of all the squares are replaced with little triangles so that when the quilt is viewed from a distance, the squares appear almost circular, like snowballs) and I cut out all the squares from my blue fabrics. I laid them out and stacked the rows in neat piles – and then the piles sat and sat in my office for months, while I tried to muster up enthusiasm for cutting out hundreds of triangles. Nothing happened until I finally let go of the snowball idea and decided that I wanted to make something simpler, something that would exploit the way in which the fabrics pooled together. Something like a swimming pool, in fact.

Once the idea of a swimming pool had clicked, inspiration flowed. I have always liked David Hockney's paintings of sunlit Californian swimming pools, with their special shade of brilliant 'Hockney blue', and when I looked at more of his work I was fascinated to see that he has also made several stunning composite pictures with Polaroid photos that look exactly like patchworks. These inspired me to create the effect of an uneven, rippling pool surface and to enclose it with a border, like the tiles around his pools.

I was also inspired by my own experience of swimming and swimming pools; I have some great memories of 'wild' swimming when young, and have always sought out outdoor pools and lidos. One of my all-time favourite books is *Waterlog* by the late Roger Deakin, a passionate outdoor swimmer whose descriptions of swimming in the moat of his ancient Suffolk house are wonderfully vivid. I have read this book many times and love his accounts of swimming with wildlife and through water containing various plants, and how he parts and clears the debris on the surface of the water as he glides along. This is why, when choosing the fabrics, I was happy to include leaves and foliage, which suggest the variety of plants that appear or fall on the surface of ponds and natural swimming pools.

design

As soon as I had moved on to the swimming pool idea, the design almost made itself. This is such a straightforward quilt to put together that it was a real pleasure simply to swim in the colours and the fabrics. It is made with 5in (12.5cm) squares (finished size), which are big enough to contain good portions of larger designs – especially whole, wavy flowers – and big enough to build up a colour story quickly and effectively. It grew to large proportions, like a real pool, and I enclosed the 'water' with a medium-sized border to stop it leaking. The quilt has thirteen squares across and fifteen squares down but, like any pool, it can be made to the size you want it to be.

fabrics

All the fabric choices were dictated by the soft aqua/ blue-green palette and the fact that I wanted to create a swirling, rippling, dappled effect in which fabrics meld together (a high contrast was the opposite of what I was after). I wanted the eye to drift over the quilt as if it were the surface of a swimming pool, without seeing lines and seams, and the beginnings and ends of patterns, and this is why there are so many gently wavy and soft-focus fabrics in the quilt top. Nevertheless, I soon discovered that it was possible to introduce fabrics that are predominantly blue-green and yet have interesting colour highlights such as coral red, pink and magenta.

The fabrics I used in the quilt top include: 'Arbour', 'Potentilla', two colourways of 'Minton', 'Guinea Flowers', a hydrangea stripe from the Lille collection and Sage 'Verbena', all by Kaffe Fassett, 'Ribbons and Bows' and a vegetable print by Martha Negley, 'Morning Glory', 'Pansy', 'Banded Poppy', 'Foxgloves' and 'Coral Leaf' by Philip Jacobs, 'Eyelashes' and 'Chrysanthemum' by Amy Butler, 'Gerbera Daisy' by Carla Miller and three designs from the Flea Market Fancy collection by Denyse Schmidt.

Having created the pool effect, I then wanted a bold and definite border, just as swimming pools often have paving or edging. The striking 'Verbena' print in Cobalt by Kaffe Fassett added a dark, dramatic border to mark the edge of the pool so that people wouldn't fall in. I then wanted the binding to blend in with the border and, because I did not have enough 'Verbena', I used a mid-blue print featuring the kind of exotic flowers you might find next to a pool in Hawaii. (In fact, this was one of the fabrics that had been rejected from the quilt top because its blue was more sky blue than sea blue.)

As soon as I saw the aqua tones of 'Brocade Flowers' by Kaffe Fassett, with its suggestions of swirling water and reflected, scattered sunlight on a pool in summer, I knew I had found the perfect backing fabric. And there is no doubt that, with all these beautiful watery fabrics, putting the whole thing together was like diving into a soft, warm, dappled pool.

✂ materials

Note: This quilt can be made smaller or larger by reducing or increasing the number of squares and/ or by omitting the border (but remember to take any alterations into account when buying wadding, binding and backing fabrics).

- - - - - - - - - - - - - - - - - -

Fabric suggestions: The best way to approach a 'colour story' quilt like this is to decide on a specific shade or colour and then to buy/ collect/ recycle fabrics accordingly. It is a good colour project for someone who wants to experiment or create a quilt in a favourite colour (it is a similar colour exercise to the Purple Rain quilt on page 102, but much simpler in terms of putting together). Be fussy about the fabrics you include, but at the same time keep an open mind as to what is and is not suitable. You do need to have a few contrasts (e.g. in details or small areas of colour) to make the quilt come alive.

- - - - - - - - - - - - - - - - - -

Quilt top: The exact requirements are 4¾yd (4.3m) of fabric or 195 x 5½in (14cm) squares (excluding border – see below).

— If I were starting from scratch, I would buy ten to sixteen fabrics, bought in a mixture of ¼yd/ m and ½yd/ m pieces to make a total of 4¾yd or 4.3m.

— However, I find a better quilt is made if you bring together as many suitable fabrics as you can find without worrying about the exact total quantity. With this method, you start with twenty to twenty-five fabrics to suit the chosen colour theme; use up leftovers and small pieces of fabric that may give as few as three squares, as well as larger pieces of fabric that can yield ten squares. In my quilt, most fabrics appear around six times, although there are a couple of 'lead' or key fabrics that appear ten times and a few that appear two to three times.

— The third method is to work out exactly how many squares you need (my quilt uses 195) and cut out this number from a variety of fabrics.

Border: To make a border 7½in (19cm) wide, you will need 1⅝yd (1.5m) fabric (I would buy 2yd/ 1.8m of fabric, but you may prefer to reduce the width of the border to 7in (18cm) and to buy 1½yd/ 1.4m rather than deal with awkward measurements).

- - - - - - - - - - - - - - - - - -

Backing: Buy 5½yd/ 5m fabric (5¾yd/ 5.25m if a large repeat pattern).

- - - - - - - - - - - - - - - - - -

Binding: You will need 20in (51cm) of fabric for the binding.

- - - - - - - - - - - - - - - - - -

You will also need:

— A piece of wadding 3–4in (7.5–10cm) larger all around than the quilt top (I use 100 per cent organic cotton with scrim).
— 100 per cent cotton all-purpose sewing thread in ecru or taupe for the machine piecing.
— 100 per cent cotton quilting thread.

- - - - - - - - - - - - - - - - - -

Final measurements: 80 x 90in (203 x 228.5cm).

The quilt has thirteen squares across and fifteen down, plus a border.

directions

All seam allowances are ¼in (6mm) unless otherwise specified.

— There are two ways to begin making this quilt. Either cut out 195 x 5½in (14cm) squares or as many as you need depending on the finished size of the quilt, OR cut out a few 5½in (14cm) squares from all the potential fabrics and play with these before deciding which will be included, then cut out more batches of squares as you build up the layout of the quilt.

— The idea is to create a pool of colour with no discernible lines and angles. The best way to achieve this is firstly by having a good number of swirling, loose, flowing patterns in your fabrics and secondly by laying out the quilt as quickly and instinctively as possible, putting fabrics down in a quasi-random fashion. Make adjustments later, after looking over the quilt from different vantage points and making sure that the fabrics are evenly distributed and scattered, and that any stand-out fabrics that draw the eye are not too close together.

— Once you are happy with the layout, pick up the squares in rows or columns, working from left to right, making piles of squares. Number these piles clearly with Post-It notes pinned through the fabrics so that you know what goes where.

— Machine-piece the rows/ columns in the correct order.

— Iron each row/ column, pressing the seams to one side. Alternate the direction of the seam-pressing with each row/ column.

— Now machine-sew the rows/ columns together in the correct order to make the quilt top. Iron, pressing the seams to one side (this time they can all go in the same direction).

— Make the border by cutting out 8in (20cm) strips from your chosen fabric. If you are using a design with a clear vertical pattern, you will need to cut the fabric lengthways to get the strips or 'sashing' to go down the sides of the quilt, and widthways to get the strips for the top and bottom of the quilt. Sew the strips together to make the border pieces. Attach the side borders first and trim, then attach the top and bottom borders.

— Iron the quilt top and press the seams so that they face out towards the edge of the quilt.

— Make the backing by sewing together two full widths, 98in (249cm) long, of the backing fabric so that the backing is 3–4in (7.5–10cm) larger all around than the quilt top. Trim the selvedges first if preferred and use a ½in (1cm) seam allowance. Press the seam open and iron the back before making the quilt sandwich.

— Make the quilt sandwich (see page 142 for further details) and trim the edges so that the wadding and backing are approximately 2in (5cm) larger than the quilt top.

— Hand-quilt with cotton quilting thread. I used a deep aqua thread and quilted a criss-cross pattern of diagonal lines through the squares, and then I quilted a straight line ¼in (6mm) in from the inside edge of the border. Use masking tape to mark the lines and remove after stitching.

— Trim the quilt top with scissors or a rotary cutter.

— Make and attach the binding (see page 143 for further instructions).

— Go for a swim in your virtual pool.

More blue/ swimming pool inspiration:

Paintings by David Hockney (see www.hockneypictures.com).

Waterlog by Roger Deakin (Vintage, 2000).

charming
chintz

Years ago, I worked in the marketing department of Arthur Sanderson & Sons, the long-established English wallpaper and furnishing fabrics company. I didn't stay with the company for long, but I did come away with a taste for chintz fabrics and chintzy designs. It was there that I discovered the beauty of the shiny, freshly glazed fabrics and the swathes of gorgeous English country-house-style designs in the showroom, and it was there that my love affair with big, blowsy floral fabrics began.

So it's no wonder I am drawn to the Rowan quilting fabrics designed by Philip Jacobs (he also designs furnishing fabrics for several companies, including Sanderson). He captures the charm of chintz in lovely, large-scale designs in all sorts of beautiful colours, and it was the combination of my memories of Sanderson and Philip's fabrics that inspired me to make this chintzy quilt. In fact, all the big prints in the quilt are by Philip Jacobs because, to my mind, he designs the very best country house chintz designs, the kind of fabrics I have seen in Frogmore House in Windsor (in the grounds of the Castle and a fabulous place for chintz inspiration) and the kind you might find in National Trust properties, grand country houses or in interior shots in *Country Life* – as well as in many an ordinary living room.

These are the designs that you find on wallpapers and curtains chosen by formidable interior designers who can fill a room with chintzy style and make it work. It's a historical style that pays no attention to changing fashions or exhortations to 'chuck out the chintz'. For years, these designers have been mixing lots of lovely faded or fading, charming prints in gentle, powdery tones such as ecru and cream, deep green and red, dusky pink and old gold, cloud grey and cornflower blue. They combine large designs and small designs, botanical prints, Paisleys, sprigs and ticking, and fabrics you imagine may have come from Provence or India, France or Holland, as well as fabrics from old

English companies such as Liberty, Colefax & Fowler, and Warner.

I very much wanted to use as many of Philip's fabrics as possible to create a quilt that would not look out of place in a chintz-filled drawing room in which there are no hard, clear lines, and the upholstery, wallpaper and draperies all merge into one another to create a gentle and very genteel faded floral bower. Not that I wished to live in a bower myself, but I do like a little charming chintz in a quilt.

design

My palette, fabrics and chintz idea were sorted out long before I knew how I was going to use them. I had collected the four main, large-scale fabrics and carefully selected the complementary smaller prints to go with each one. I kept the fabrics in a pile with each small-scale print folded inside its larger partner, and I would often bring them out to look at them for inspiration as to how I was going to get them into a quilt. But nothing happened. Then, just as I was beginning to think an idea would never click, I looked around at the quilts I'd made before with a deliberately vintage, old-fashioned feel and saw that small squares worked every time.

There is something about an abundance of small squares that brings to mind beautifully

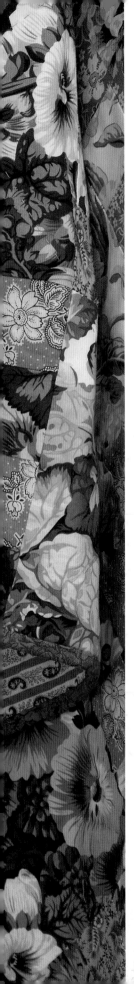

dense and interesting hand-sewn quilts made with small-detail fabrics, and I imagined this would work well to create the feel of a busy, over-furnished and upholstered drawing room shrine to chintz. But I still wanted to show off the big botanical prints, so I decided to alternate each sixteen-patch square with a plain square. I reckoned the larger 8in (20cm) squares would be big enough to show off the floral patterns, and I already knew that the alternating blocks made of sixteen 2in (5cm) squares would create the vintage look I wanted. I liked the idea of squares making up one large square, so I made the quilt with eight blocks across and eight down. (This is a mathematically very regular quilt, all based on multiples of 2, 4, 8 and 16.) I decided to use the large patterns in the small squares, too, so that there would be a melding and elision of fabrics suggesting layer upon layer of gloriously chintzy flowers.

So I sewed my sets of blocks, plain and sixteen-patch, and thought of scattering them or creating an Irish Chain type of pattern. In the end, though, I kept them in two-fabric rows and ran them in colour sequences, with each row repeated twice within a set pattern (see diagram on page 135). I found it difficult to place the rows, so I took photos of different layouts and uploaded them to help me decide (a reverse magnifying glass would work well and take less time).

I decided that this particular quilt did not need a border, as I felt a border would detract from the quilt's 'busyness' and its pleasantly cluttered look (although a different version could look great with a border).

fabrics

All four of the main floral fabrics are designed by Philip Jacobs (see page 136), because I love the sense of scale and drama and the beautiful palettes in his fabrics. For each main fabric, I found a complementary small-scale design in my collection of fabrics, and it was fascinating to see how pairs could be made using similar or matching colours and motifs. The fabrics I used are 'Blowsey' in Natural with a grey Yuwa 'Live Life' print, 'Tall Hollyhock' in Natural with a dusty-pink Kokka 'Coccinelle' print, 'Geranium' in Natural with one of the 'A Little Bird Told Me' fabrics from Windham, and finally 'Luscious' in Natural and a second Windham reproduction fabric.

I consulted Susie Green of Duxhurst Quilting (www.duxhurstquilting.co.uk) about the backing and she suggested a reproduction Paisley ticking and it works perfectly with the densely patterned top; it is also the kind of fabric you might have found in rooms filled with period chintz. It is from the Rocky Mountain Quilt Museum collection by Judie Rothermel for Marcus Fabrics.

I wanted the binding to create a firm, clear outline to hold the flowers in and to stop them spilling over, so used a deep emerald and black etched-flower fabric that I'd bought years ago (no information on the selvedge, but this type of fabric is widely available).

More suitable fabrics for this type of quilt:
- Philip Jacobs and Martha Negley create lovely chintzy-style, large-scale floral fabrics.
- Anna Griffin designs beautiful big botanical prints for Windham.
- Windham also produce a range of exquisite small-scale vintage/ reproduction fabrics, which would work well with larger designs.
- Kokka and Yuwa both have lovely blowsy flower collections.

materials

Fabric suggestions: Choose four big, floral prints – the botanical illustration style on a pale background works best – and then choose a small-scale fabric to complement each one. To achieve the vintage chintz look, you will need to keep to a fairly restricted colour palette. Alternatively, simply use as many lovely chintzy fabrics as you like with both large- and small-scale designs.

Quilt top: You will need ¾yd/ m of each of the four main large-scale floral fabrics, plus a 10in (25cm) piece of each of the four complementary small-scale patterns (e.g. Paisley, sprigs, small flowers, and reproduction American Civil War and vintage designs).

Backing/ binding: The backing takes 4yd/ m of fabric and the binding takes 16in (40.5cm) or ½yd/ m of a contrasting fabric.

You will also need:

— A piece of wadding 3–4in (7.5–10cm) larger all around than the quilt top (I use 100 per cent organic cotton with scrim).
— 100 per cent cotton all-purpose sewing thread in ecru or taupe for the machine piecing.
— 100 per cent cotton quilting thread for machine or hand quilting.

Finished measurements: 65 x 65in (165 x 165cm).

directions

This quilt is very straightforward. Once you have decided on the fabrics, you can cut out all the pieces before laying out the design. If it is hard to decide which fabrics to use, cut out a few small squares of each and play with them before making your selection.

Quick method: If you are absolutely sure about the fabrics, it is possible to make this quilt without laying it all out in advance. Cut out the large squares and put to one side. Then cut out the small squares. Now make the four sets of eight two-fabric, sixteen-patch squares. Sew together the blocks in rows, then join the rows together to make the top (see diagram). All dimensions are given below.

Longer method (the one I use, because I like to see everything set out before I begin to sew):

— All seam allowances are ¼in (6mm) unless otherwise stated.

— This quilt is made up of sixty-four 8in (20cm) squares (finished): thirty-two single-fabric squares (eight per fabric) and thirty-two sixteen-patch squares (eight each of four two-colour blocks).

— Cut out eight 8½in (21.5cm) squares from each of the four main fabrics (1–4).

— Cut out sixty-four 2½in (6cm) squares from each of the four main fabrics.

— Cut out sixty-four 2½in (6cm) squares from each of the four complementary fabrics (A–D).

— Note: Keep the patterns/ flowers all facing the right way up. One reason for laying out the quilt before sewing is to make sure all the fabrics are placed correctly – you do not want upside-down geraniums to spoil the effect (unless it's deliberate).

— Now make the sixteen-patch blocks (i.e. a square made up of sixteen smaller squares), alternating the two fabrics in a chequerboard pattern (see diagram).

— To make a block, bring the sixteen squares to the sewing machine and arrange them in the correct order before sewing. Sew the pairs of squares together, two per row, then sew the pairs of squares together to create four rows (chain-piece to make this process faster).

— Press each row, pressing the seams in alternating directions.

— Sew the four rows together to make the square block.

— Iron each block, pressing all the seams in the same direction.

— Now lay out the blocks and plain squares, following the diagram or according to your own design.

— Sew the blocks together to make the rows and press all the seams to one side, alternating direction with each row.

— Now sew the rows together to make the quilt top. Iron and press all the seams in the same direction.

— Make the backing by sewing together two widths of fabric 72in (183cm) long with a ½in (1cm) seam. (The back needs to be 3–4in/ 7.5–10cm larger all around than the top.) Iron the back and press open the seam.

— Make the quilt sandwich (see page 142 for further instructions) and trim the wadding and backing so that it is 2in (5cm) larger all around than the quilt top.

— Machine- or hand-quilt the quilt. I used Mettler quilting thread in old gold and stitched a criss-cross pattern of diagonal lines (using strips of masking tape to mark the lines).

— Trim the quilt edges and attach the binding (see page 143 for further instructions).

— Throw the quilt over a chair or sofa and take tea as if you were in a chintz-filled drawing room in a lovely old English country house.

Further chintz inspiration:

The Floral Home by Leslie Geddes-Brown (Mitchell-Beazley, 1992).

Frogmore House, Windsor (open to the public twice a year: see www.royalcollection.org.uk).

There are two types of block: a plain square (fabrics 1–4), and a two-colour sixteen-patch block (A +1, B + 2, C + 3, D + 4).

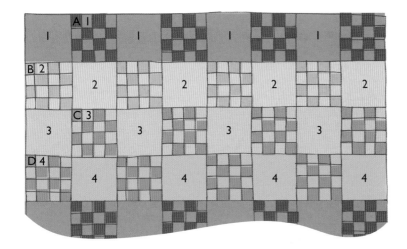

The quilt has eight blocks across and eight blocks down.

fabric inspiration

philip jacobs

From the very first moment I saw them, Philip Jacobs's fabrics made a huge impression on me; with their richness and lush colours, they are like walking into a hot-house or conservatory, or taking a stroll along a densely planted herbaceous border. They reminded me immediately of Victorian interiors depicted in great detail and rich colour in the paintings of the time, and of photographs of twentieth-century country house drawing rooms filled with floral chintzes.

So I was intrigued to find out more about these bold and unusual designs that break the mould of quilt fabrics and take them into a new realm of scale and effect. It came as no surprise to discover that Philip has been a designer of furnishing fabrics for many years, ever since he left art college in 1976 with a degree in textiles and fashion, and to find out that he is well known in that world for his amazing floral designs based on nineteenth-century French and English documents and archives. He made his first designs for the quilting market in 2004 after a visit from Kaffe Fassett, who felt that his trademark large-scale florals, full of colour and depth, would translate well into fabric for quilts. And although some quilters may initially baulk at the sheer size of the flowers and repeats, and the use of the unusual and luscious colours, they are indeed perfect for quilts in that they cut up beautifully (often giving wonderful surprises) and they look amazing in large pieces or on quilt backs. (See the Russian Shawl quilt, page 56, for an example.)

What excites Philip about designing fabrics for patchwork and quilting is that it offers a different format to the one he works with on furnishing fabrics. Although he has always loved designing sumptuous and dense fabrics, he can also play with areas of space within flowers when creating fabrics that might hang as curtains or cover a chair, but for patchwork the designs need to have a good all-over coverage, otherwise there is the possibility of ending up with a patch or set of patches that are devoid of pattern. Plus there is the additional reward of seeing how quilters use them, and how they manage to produce endless variations with them. In fact, he says that seeing a well-made quilt induces a similar feeling to the one he experiences when he looks at a beautiful old Persian rug glowing with texture and colour.

As for inspiration, Philip is completely surrounded by it. His Dorset studio and barn is full to bursting with his vast archive and collection of eighteenth-, nineteenth- and twentieth-century fabrics and wallpapers. He also believes, like many an artist or writer, that inspiration just happens; for him, the more ideas he works on, the more just seem to appear.

Philip is steeped in textile history and is an authority on the subject, which is why his fabrics are so clever and stunning. His real passion is for English and French fabrics of the mid-nineteenth century, a period that saw, as Philip puts it, a 'great flowering' in floral design. This was as a direct result of Victorian explorers and plant collectors who brought back a variety of exotic and unknown plants for the new botanical gardens and houses such as Kew. These were then grown in the gardens of the period, and consequently began to appear in fabric and wallpaper design. Philip is constantly amazed that everyone knows about William Morris and the Arts and Crafts movement later in the century, but hardly anyone knows about the 1850s as the high point for woodblock-printed floral fabric, even though it was this technique that Morris explored and developed.

Philip usually starts a new collection with a few rough drawings on a scrap of paper. When planning a collection, he tries to have a balance of different scales and formats; so there may be an epic, over-the-top floral, a spaced floral trail with plenty of background, a few very dense designs done in his own individual stylized way, sometimes a floral stripe and a smaller leaf design, and perhaps also a tropical-style jungle print and a design influenced by the Arts and Crafts movement. He is never short of ideas and happily finds that the more ideas and designs he produces, the more the inspiration flows. Once he has achieved a successful layout, he then tries the same format with different flowers, knowing that the possibilities are endless. After Philip has painted up a whole group of designs, he and Kaffe Fassett meet up to make a selection for the final collection.

The creative process is very simple and very traditional. Philip uses paper, pencil, gouache paint, paintbrushes and tracing paper, but no computer. However, he does use a photocopier to help plan the layouts. He takes colours from old textile documents which, due to their age, often have a fantastic richness and patina to them, something he is happy to reproduce (Philip also makes good use of the maximum number of seventeen colours that can be used when printing quilt fabric), while Kaffe works on the brighter, more contemporary colourways.

When I asked Philip how he manages to come up with so many variations on a design and still make each one covetable and gorgeous, he answered that it really is the result of years of practice and experience; with any art, constant practice makes it appear almost effortless to the beholder. An American textile manufacturer, Harry Hinson, once said to him, 'Each design has to be so beautiful that people just have to have it', and he has tried to follow that philosophy (and it works every time for me).

Philip undoubtedly deserves recognition for his unique approach to designing fabrics for quilts and for breathing new life into old patterns and designs so that we do not lose sight of our textile heritage. Every time we use one of his designs, we are stitching a little piece of textile history into our quilts.

starting out: the basics

In this section you will find directions, tips and ideas for making quilts. These are my personal methods that I have developed over time. Of course, there are all sorts of ways to make quilts, and you may find that my approach is quite different or contrary to that of other books and quilters, but it is rooted in the firm conviction that making quilts should be straightforward and enjoyable, and not a matter of following a large set of rigid rules. As a result, I have discarded quite a lot of the accepted wisdom and techniques, and simplified the whole process as much as possible.

I do not work with foundation piecing, strip piecing, hand piecing or appliqué, so you won't find instructions for those techniques here. But you will find what I hope are useful, down-to-earth, pragmatic ideas for making machine-pieced and hand-quilted quilts.

First, let's look at the essential equipment and techniques needed to make simple but beautiful quilts.

equipment checklist

This is what you will need in addition to fabric and filling (see Decisions, Decisions, page 15, for more details):

— An iron with good steam action: an iron is a quilter's best friend and can sort out a multitude of minor problems.

— A large pair of scissors for general fabric cutting: tie a length of ribbon or sew a name-tape around the handle for clear identification (fabric scissors should not be used on other materials such as paper, as this blunts them).

— A pair of small, very sharp scissors for snipping threads and undoing sewing mistakes (keep next to the sewing machine or close by when quilting).

— A rotary cutter (and a spare blade or two) for cutting out quilt pieces: the two best-known brands are Fiskars and Olfa, and both are excellent. Handle and use with care as the blades are lethal.

— A self-healing mat (the largest you can afford/ store): mine is a modest 17 x 23in (43 x 58cm), which is fine; I have found that anything smaller can make it difficult to cut out large pieces.

— A couple of quilting rulers: I love my Creative Grids© rulers because they have a very useful half-inch edge (instead of measuring only in full inches). I use a large square (15½ x 15½in), a smaller square (10½ x 10½in) and a long rectangle (7½ x 23½in) for virtually all my quilts.

— Sewing machine: nothing fancy is needed, just a reliable model with a presser foot that measures ¼in (6mm) from the needle to the outside edge so that you can use this as your guide when sewing ¼in (6mm) seams. My machine is a basic but sturdy, second-hand, twenty-five-year-old Bernina Nova.

— All-purpose, 100 per cent cotton thread in neutral colours, such as ecru or taupe, for machine piecing (I use Gutermann).

— Post-It notes for numbering piles or rows of fabrics.

— A box of long, glass-headed quilter's pins; a pincushion.

— Masking tape for marking quilting lines when hand-quilting.

— Quilting thread in 100 per cent cotton: Mettler threads are wonderful if you can find them, Gutermann threads are widely available, or you can use DMC/ Anchor cotton embroidery thread.

— Needles for hand quilting: special quilting needles are thin and short. I use size 8 quilting needles; alternatively, size 8 embroidery needles or size 8 sharps, as I like a longer needle, although any slim needle will be fine.

— A thimble to wear on the second finger of the hand in which you hold a needle: I prefer close-fitting leather thimbles, as metal ones seem to fall off my finger all the time.

preparation

I pre-wash all cotton fabrics. Some quilters do not bother with this step, but I prefer to for several reasons:

- First, there's the risk of dye running in a fabric. With good-quality quilting fabrics, this happens rarely these days, but I would much rather lose a fabric at the pre-wash stage than have the horror of it running into a finished quilt when I wash it.

- Then there is the issue of shrinkage (generally calculated to be approximately 2 per cent), and I like to get this out of the way before I begin cutting, rather than sew up fabrics that could, potentially, shrink at different rates once they are in a quilt.

- The main reason, though, is that all fabrics have 'size' (a very thin layer of gelatinous paste) applied to them before they leave the factory; this adds body and sheen and it is what makes new fabrics feel so crisp and smooth. It comes off in the first wash, leaving a fabric with the slightly softer, more 'used' feel that I prefer.

- Finally, I find that pre-washed fabrics stick together better when it comes to piecing on the sewing machine.

If you decide to pre-wash, do so in a low-temperature, short-cycle wash (max. 30°C). Take the washed fabrics out and give them a good shake before folding and drying on a drying rack. I used to dry mine on a washing line, but found that pegging out fabrics can pull them out of shape. As soon as the fabrics are dry or nearly dry, fold and stack them neatly before ironing. It makes me laugh that I, normally so averse to folding and ironing, am a real stickler for this when it comes to my quilting fabrics. It may sound fussy, but if you leave very dry cotton fabrics scrunched up in a pile, it can be incredibly difficult to eradicate the creases when you come to iron. Store ironed and folded fabrics out of direct sunlight. Although most fabrics are pretty light-fast, it can be annoying to unfold a favourite piece and find you have sun-bleached fold marks across it.

cutting and piecing

- You need to know how to use a rotary cutter with a quilting ruler and self-healing mat. Although fabrics can be cut out with scissors, a rotary cutter does an infinitely better, far quicker and more accurate job, gives super-straight, neat edges and allows you to cut through up to four layers of fabric at a time. It is one technique I would recommend that you learn by

having someone show you, as there is nothing better (and safer) than having a session with someone who is practised with a rotary cutter. Alternatively, there are some useful videos on the Internet that demonstrate rotary cutting (look on YouTube or Instructables). Remember to always cut away from you and to keep the blade locked at all times when the cutter is not in use.

- When it comes to piecing (i.e. sewing the parts of a quilt together), you do not need to pin or tack the fabrics beforehand. Just feed the fabrics, right sides together and with the edges accurately aligned, as you sew them. This goes against all the teachings of needlework lessons, I know, but pinning really is not necessary. (Even slippery silks and wools can be sewn without pinning, but this does take a little more patience.) Light cottons have enough fibres on the surface to hold the pieces lightly together as you feed them under the needle. Occasionally, when sewing two long rows of blocks together, I may pin in a few places to make sure the seams are aligned, and to make it easier to handle the pieces of fabric at the sewing machine.

- Like all quilters, I use ¼in (6mm) seams for all piecing (the one exception is when I use a ½in/ 12mm seam for the backing). A seam of ¼in (6mm) may not seem like a lot, but it does work as long as you use non-frayed fabrics and keep the raw edges of the pieces very carefully aligned as they go under the needle.

There is no need to do any backstitching at the beginning or end of a seam – just cut the loose threads leaving a 1–2in (2.5–5cm) tail – because each seam is later intersected, crossed and sewn over, and secured when the piece is sewn to its neighbours. (Just turn over a finished quilt top and you will see the network of seams that holds the whole thing together.)

Chain piecing is very useful when you are putting together a large quantity of pairs of pieces, for example squares, to make up larger squares (see Postage Stamp, page 94 and Charming Chintz, page 130), when it would be time-consuming to raise the presser foot and cut threads after every square. Simply feed the pieces one after the other under the foot, allowing the machine to do a few stitches in the air before moving on to the next piece. (I thought this might break the needle, but I can assure you it works.)

Once you get used to handling cotton quilting fabrics, you will discover that they have quite a degree of 'give' or stretch. This is very useful when, for example, you find that seams are not matching perfectly and it is possible to do a little pulling to get sides to match. When sewing, keep the needle down and manipulate the top or bottom fabrics gently as necessary. Or pull gently, pin and then sew.

Iron seams as you go along, for example when you have made a block (see Purple Rain, page 102) or a row (see Floral Frocks, page 88) and before moving on to the next. Some quilters open out every seam; others press seams to one side. I iron to one side all the time; the only exceptions are the main seams on the backing fabric, which I open out, and when I am working with thicker fabrics such as wool, which would make a ridge if pressed to one side (see Suits and Ties, page 40).

It's important to iron the seams in a certain direction according to how they meet the next row or block – it is preferable not to join seams pressed to the same side, as this gives four layers of fabric and creates ridges in the quilt. So, for example, in the Charming Chintz quilt (see page 130), I ironed the top row so that all the seams that join the large squares and the sixteen-square blocks faced to the left, then the seams on the row underneath faced to the right, and the row beneath that to the left, and so on.

My more relaxed approach to quilting also means that I don't bother trimming edges of pieces, rows, blocks or even whole quilts after sewing, because this causes a lot of extra work and I am always nervous that I might cut too much off. If you do find you have a block or row that is looking decidedly raggedy at the edge, all you need to do is sew it to the next block or row with a straight line, and no one will ever see the less-than-perfect edge.

The same applies to the outer edge of the quilt; if you can sew the binding on in as straight a line as possible, it will hide a multitude of previous sins. Personally, I do not mind if the finished outer edge is not plumb-straight and has a slight wiggle to it. If this does bother you, trim the edge with a rotary cutter and ruler. But be careful: it's very easy to get carried away with neatening and to over-trim and spoil the balance and design (it's rather like trying to straighten the edge of a cheesecake so that no one can tell you've been picking – you find yourself going back to the fridge over and over again).

- Liza Prior Lucy gave me a brilliant piece of advice about making quilt tops with long seams (along rows or strips). It is very important that you alternate the direction in which you sew long seams; if you sew long seams from, say, top to bottom every time, there is a danger of the square or rectangle ending up more like a parallelogram. So you need to start at one end and then begin the next seam at the opposite end, in order to balance the tension of the stitching. (Think of it as making a U-turn at the end of a road.) I use a pin each time to mark the end I need to start from next – it's amazing how quickly you can forget.

- When sewing the lengths of fabric to make a quilt backing, I use ½in (12mm) seams, then open them out and iron them flat. You may want to trim off the selvedge first, but I find it's not absolutely necessary.

putting a quilt together: making the quilt sandwich

In terms of techniques and process, we now have a quilt top and a backing. The next step is to make a 'quilt sandwich': top, wadding or filling, and backing. The aim is to make all three layers as smooth as possible.

- Lay out the backing fabric (right side down) on the carpet, a bed or on a large table (secure with bulldog clips). Now lay the wadding or filling on top and, working from the centre, smooth it until all wrinkles and creases have been removed. (Check the packaging for the wadding to find out whether there is a right and wrong side, and whether you need to iron, hang or smooth out the sheet before putting it in the sandwich.) If the wadding is much larger than the backing, trim with scissors so that both are more or less the same size. Next, place the quilt top, right side up, on the top of the sandwich layers. Match main or central seams and make sure it is lying within the framework of the backing/ wadding before pinning.

- I pin the sandwich together with large, glass-headed quilter's pins, pinning every 5–6in (12–15cm) – which takes a lot of pins. I start from the centre and work out to the sides, or sometimes from one end to the other, constantly smoothing the fabric and adjusting the backing to stop wrinkles forming. Some quilters prefer to use large quilting safety pins (I tried this, but I found they moved the fabric too much when fastening), and many also tack the sandwich after pinning. Call me reckless, but I am happy with a pinned quilt, even though it

does have to be handled with care. Warn others that the quilt is prickly or, better still, keep it out of reach until the pins have been removed.

- Trim the edges of excess backing and wadding, but do not trim right to the edge of the quilt top, as quilts can still move or need to be slightly adjusted as you quilt. I leave a 3–4in (7.5–10cm) excess around the edge, which is cut off after quilting.

Note: You may want to ask someone with a long-arm quilter to make the sandwich and tack it together before handing it back to you to hand-quilt and bind (you may also want her to machine-quilt and bind the quilt). This is a marvellous service if you are short of space or have difficulty achieving a really smooth, flat sandwich.

quilting

I hand-quilt my quilts on my lap without a hoop or frame. This is why and how:

- I like the effect of hand quilting more than that of machine quilting, but this is a personal preference. I feel it makes a quilt look fuller and less flattened, and gives it an attractive, hand-made appearance.

- I like the simplicity of straight lines and the fact that you can see the stitches quite clearly. I use relatively large running stitches in straight lines, but I sometimes adjust and make shorter stitches if the fabric pieces are smaller, for example on the Postage Stamp quilt (page 94).

- I use a wadding that allows me to leave quite large spaces between quilting lines, should I wish (up to

20cm/ 8in) – the 'scrim' holds the fabrics in place (see Decisions, Decisions, page 15).

— For line guidance, I often simply follow the seams of the quilt top, sewing about ¼in (6mm) away from the lines so that I am not trying to get the needle through too many layers of fabric. But if I want to create diagonal lines or lines away from seams, I use masking tape to mark a line and stitch along this before pulling it off gently. I don't use any marker pens or stencils.

— Even king-sized quilts can be hand-quilted on your lap without a hoop while sitting on a settee. You simply need to spread out and work methodically from one side or end to the other, smoothing and flattening as you go along.

— Hand quilting is quicker to do than you may think and it's possible to quilt a single-bed-sized quilt in three or four evenings. It creates the perfect excuse to watch plenty of excellent films.

There are alternative methods for holding a quilt sandwich together. Of course, it can be machine-quilted (instructions can be found in plenty of good quilting books or on the Internet), but have you thought about tying the quilt at regular intervals, or using buttons to bring the three layers together? Both techniques create lovely effects. And hand quilting does not have to be simple running stitch – it can be more decorative stitching such as herringbone or feather stitch, or perhaps stars at the intersections of squares.

Once a quilt has been quilted, cut off the excess fabric so that all three parts of the sandwich are the same size. If desired, straighten the edges with a rotary cutter and ruler (I don't do this).

binding

For a long time, I used four strips (one for each edge) attached in order, and simply tucked under the ends and stitched them in place. I now know how to do continuous binding (using one long piece and folding it to create mitred corners – although I don't cut it on the bias), but any type of binding method is fine if it works for the quilt and quilter.

To make a continuous binding, cut and join strips to achieve the appropriate length – I use 2½in (6cm) strips – and sew them together with a ¼in (6mm) seam. Press the seams open, then fold and iron the binding in half to make a long, double-thickness strip. Starting at the bottom right-hand corner and with a ¼in (6mm) seam, machine the raw edge to the quilt top. Fold the binding over and handstitch in place on the back of the quilt. For a tutorial in making neat mitred corners, look on YouTube.

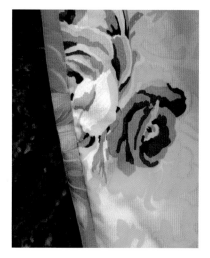

finishing

Once you have created a lovely quilt, you may want to sew on a personalized label or a label that gives the name of the quilt and the year of making and/ or take a few photographs (especially if you are giving it away). Now use and enjoy your quilt!

quilting workspace

Much as I would love a room dedicated to quilting, I don't have one. This means that I have had to solve the various problems that many quilters face when making quilts in small, shared spaces.

Of course, it is possible to work on one strip or row or block at a time, building up the quilt from your seat in front of the sewing machine. If you have the ability to hold designs in your mind while you sew and to visualize how the blocks will work together, this at-the-machine approach will work. But if, like me, you prefer to lay out the pieces for a whole quilt top before sewing them together, you need to find or make as much space as possible.

Here are some tips for meeting the challenges of small-space quilting:

Use the biggest floor space available, preferably carpeted

If you lay out fabric pieces on a wooden or tiled floor, they will blow everywhere if there's a draught. Bedrooms, living rooms or large hallways are best, and you can then use a bed, chair, settee or the stairs as a viewing platform to get a good overall view of the quilt (but make sure you do this from more than one angle, end or side).

Lay out and pick up in one day

This is not ideal, as it really does pay to revisit a quilt a few times and in different lights before you begin to sew up, even if it just means leaving the quilt overnight and looking at it again in the morning. If your time is very limited, you could lay out the pieces, photograph the layout with a digital camera, and then pick up the pieces in rows, columns or blocks, numbering each one as you go along with Post-It notes pinned to the piles. Upload the photos on to the computer, enlarge them and look carefully to see what is working and what is not. If the design needs alterations, you can lay it out again and make changes before putting it back into labelled piles and moving on to the sewing.

Alternatively, lay out the quilt on a large piece of brushed cotton or flannel, spread out on the floor or hung on the wall

The quilt fabric will stick to the flannel, which can be carefully folded or rolled and brought out again when the carpet, floor or wall space is clear.

Do not walk on laid-out quilt pieces in socks

Make sure that everyone else in the house knows not to, as well. Cotton fabric sticks to socks and can be walked about, creating quilt chaos.

Use a bed for laying out quilt pieces

If you are really stuck for space, the biggest bed in the house is the best place to work. Strip the bed so that you have a flat surface. Alternatively, cover the mattress with a pale brushed cotton sheet or large piece of cotton flannel; the quilt pieces will stick to the sheet/ flannel, which can then be folded carefully and stored/ brought out when required.

A bed is also a good place for doing the sandwiching part (see page 142). Pin the edges of the backing fabric, right side down, to the mattress, place the wadding or filling on top and then the quilt top (right side up).

Use a design board

I have used a design board at a quilt workshop, and it's a brilliant solution to the space problem, plus it allows you to stand back and scrutinize your quilt design. It is also good for quilters whose knees and backs protest at working on the floor. The board (or 'wall') should be covered in brushed cotton/ cotton flannel in a neutral colour – pieces of fabric will stick to it almost miraculously. A board can be something as simple as a large piece of hardboard propped up against a wall, with a brushed cotton/ cotton flannel sheet stapled on. Or, if you are handy with the toolbox or know someone who is, you can make a large folding screen, in two or three pieces, covered with flannel. Instructions for making a board or wall can be found on the Internet (search for 'quilt design board' or 'quilt design wall'). Alternatively, buy a ready-made design board/ wall from a specialist supplier.

Please do not be put off by lack of space

Quilters are renowned for their ingenuity and commitment, and there are many wonderful stories of quilters who have overcome similar challenges and problems in very overcrowded spaces. Read about the quilters of Gee's Bend if you are in need of inspiration; they will remind you that if you really want to make a quilt, a solution to space problems can always be found.

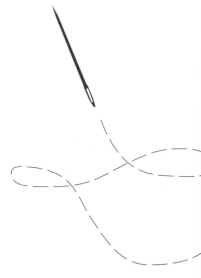

glossary

This brief glossary serves as a reminder of terms used in this book, most of which are standard terms.

BLOCK In quilt-making, blocks are basic units which are sewn together to make up a pieced quilt top.

FOUR-PATCH A block made up of four equal squares (blocks may also be nine-patch or sixteen-patch etc).

FUSSY-CUT To fussy-cut is to cut out or round a specific motif (eg flowers) or section (eg stripes) of a fabric so that the piece features it.

ON POINT Sometimes a square block is set 'on point' This means that it is set with the corners at north, south, west and east.

QUILT SANDWICH The three layers of a quilt: the quilt top, wadding and backing.

QUILT TOP The top layer of a quilt sandwich. The backing is the bottom or underneath layer, with wadding (or 'batting) in the middle.

SASHING Strips of fabric used between pieced blocks, or as a border.

WADDING Also known as batting, wadding is the middle layer of a quilt sandwich (see above).

quilt gallery

The following pages show flat shots of all the quilts featured in the book. Please note that these are not to scale, but they do give a clear indication of structure, pattern and any repeats. Each shot can be used for guidance or as a starting point; simply colour in the squares, rectangles, strips and diamonds with lovely fabrics and colours to make your own beautiful creations.

Lisbon Tile (dark)
54 × 62½in (137 × 158.5cm)

Lisbon Tile (pale)
54 × 62½in (137 × 158.5cm)

Beach Hut (Candy)
56½ × 72½in (143.5 × 184cm)

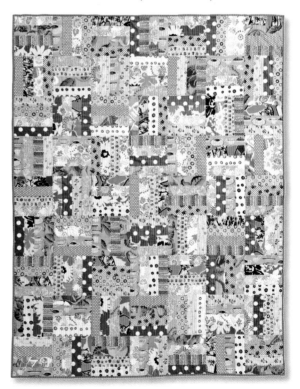

Beach Hut (Ice-Cream)
56½ × 72½in (143.5 × 184cm)

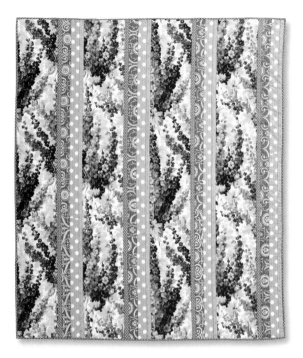

Hammock (Summer Day)
60 × 69in (152 × 175cm)

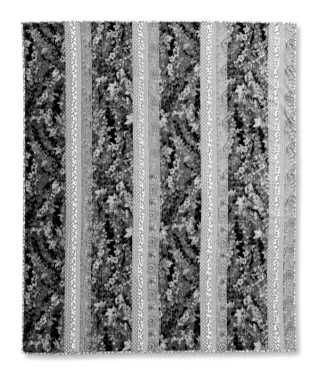

Hammock (Summer Evening)
60 × 69in (152 × 175cm)

Suits and Ties
53 × 65in (134.5 × 165cm)

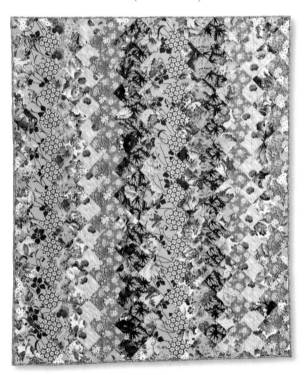

Hydrangea
61½ × 74½in (156 × 189cm)

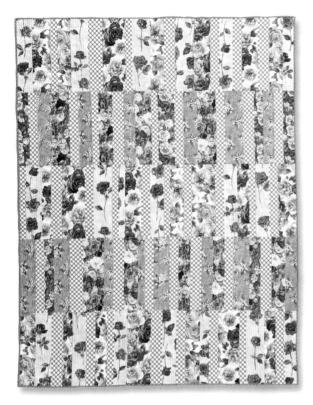

Floral Frocks
62 × 80in (157.5 × 203cm)

Amaryllis
63½ × 81in (162 × 206cm)

Postage Stamp
66 × 66in (167.5 × 167.5cm)

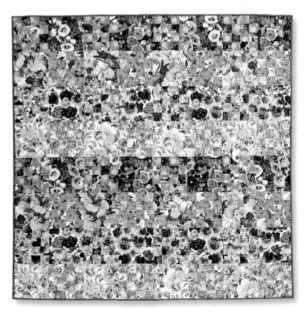

Charming Chintz
65 × 65in (165 × 165cm)

Tulip Field
86½ × 89in (220 × 226cm)

Green, Green Grass of Home
80 × 104in (203 × 264cm)

Russian Shawl (Shawl)
70 × 70in (178 × 178cm)

Russian Shawl (Matryoshka)
70 × 70in (178 × 178cm)

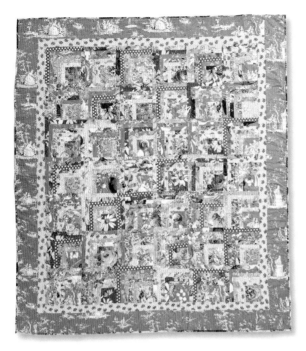

Purple Rain
66 x 75½in (167.5 x 192cm)

Swimming Pool
80 x 90in (203 x 228.5cm)

Sample Book
69 x 87in (175 x 221cm)

Ball Gown
86 x 76½in (218.5 x 194cm)

My favourite inspirational quilting books

These are the books that inspired me and helped me to get started with quilt-making. Immerse yourself in the following titles:

- *Patchwork* by Diana Lodge (Mitchell Beazley, 1994). The first quilting book I ever bought: it fuelled many early patchwork daydreams with its variety of lovely, traditional, hand-made quilts in soft and gentle colours.

- Then I discovered *Patchwork* by Kaffe Fassett and Liza Prior Lucy (Ebury, 1997), and the world of colourful quilts was opened up. This book provided the impetus to finally get started. It's the first of a trio of books from Ebury, which have inspired me over and over again. The other two titles are *Passionate Patchwork* (2001) by Kaffe Fassett and Liza Prior Lucy, and Kaffe Fassett's *V&A Quilts* (2005).

- *Successful Scrap Quilts from Simple Rectangles*, by Judy Turner and Margaret Rolfe (That Patchwork Place, 2002), is an incredibly useful book for the beginner, with masses of ideas for making effective and interesting quilts with rectangles. It gives a beginner-quilter the confidence to play with geometric and optical effects.

- *Cotton Candy Quilts*, by Mary Mashuta (C&T Publishing, 2001), introduced me to feedsack fabrics and simple, colourful, cheerful quilts, and inspired my first design efforts using pretty rather than startling fabrics. Mary Mashuta is a reliable and knowledgeable quilter who can always be trusted.

- *American Quilt Classics* by Patricia Cox (Collins & Brown, 2001). What would I give to own some of the quilts in Patricia Cox's collection? A lovely book to remind the reader of the enduring appeal of traditional, time-honoured designs.

- *Quilts*, by Denyse Schmidt (Chronicle Books, 2005), offers a fascinating contrast to Patricia Cox's book. It shows how to make ultra-modern, often strikingly plain quilts, and inspired me to envisage quilts in my own, individual way and to apply my own style for the first time.

- *Last-Minute Patchwork + Quilted Gifts*, by Joelle Hoverson (ST Craft, 2007), is written by the owner of Purl and Purl Patchwork, my favourite yarn and fabric shops in New York. Joelle has the most amazing taste and style, and proves that quilting projects need not take forever and a day to make.

- *The Quilts of Gee's Bend*, by John Beardsley et al. (Tinwood Books, 2002), and *Gee's Bend: The Architecture of the Quilt*, by Paul Arnett et al. (Tinwood Books, 2006), are two huge, beautifully illustrated books that inspired me to loosen up and simply try out my own ideas without worrying about less-than-perfect results. They taught me that it's the creative impulse and the quilt narratives that matter more than precision and neatness.

- *Patchwork Style* by Suzuko Koseki (Shambhala Publications, 2009). Japanese patchwork and quilting books are phenomenal – full of vibrant creativity and stunning, fresh new ideas – and are worth looking at just for the photos. Fortunately this, my favourite, has now been translated into English.

My favourite inspirational non-quilting books

These are where I discover more ideas: I find all sorts of inspiration, from colour combinations to potential patterns, in a wide range of books and magazines. The following are particularly good sources of ideas:

- *Amy Butler's Midwest Modern*, by Amy Butler (Stewart, Tabori & Chang, 2007), is full of ideas for living with fabric and how to put it all together. The details are beautiful.

- *Russian Textiles: Printed Cloth for the Bazaars of Central Asia*, by Susan Meller (Abrams, 2007), is a riot of fabulous red fabrics and overblown flowers that reaffirms my love affair with brazenness.

- Interiors books that feature lovely homes are not just pretty eye-candy – they also have dozens of photos of wonderful textiles and quilts, plus clever ways of using both. *Bazaar Style* by Selina Lake (Ryland Peters & Small, 2008) is a particular favourite, but I confess I love all the Ryland Peters & Small interiors books. I turn to *Vintage Fabric Style* by Lucinda Ganderton (2003) and *Flea Market Style* by Emily Chalmers (2005) when in need of a little quilting fillip.

- Japanese craft and quilt books are another source of glorious visual inspiration (and their detailed, graphic instructions are actually quite easy to follow). They offer a very contemporary approach to quilts, with unusual and surprising pattern and colour combinations that can prompt new ideas. Use the pages in English on Amazon Japan (www.amazon.co.jp) and YesAsia (www.yesasia.com). A number of sellers on eBay also offer a good selection of Japanese books and fabrics.

- Long before I started quilting, I fell in love with Designers' Guild fabrics, and now I wish the company would produce a range of patchwork-weight fabrics in the same designs. Until that happens, the next best things are the colour-and-style-saturated books by Tricia Guild published by Quadrille (*Inspiration*, *Flowers* and *Think Colour*).

- When it comes to magazines, I restrict myself to a handful of titles. *Selvedge* caters for readers with an interest in world textiles and is quite unique and special. I also find plenty of inspiration in *World of Interiors* and British *Country Living*.

- Gardening books never fail to inspire enthusiasm for colour and floral fabrics, and they often suggest possible designs (I find gardeners often think along the same lines as quilters when it comes to layouts and filling in spaces). Sarah Raven's books, such as *The Bold and Brilliant Garden* and *The Cutting Garden* (both published by Frances Lincoln), have opened up a new way of thinking about colour combinations.

- And, finally, art books can always be relied upon to kick-start quilt musings when you are low on inspiration. I find books with reproductions of works by Winifred Nicholson, Stanley Spencer, Henri Matisse, Eric Ravilious, Vanessa Bell and artists of the Victorian period always get the creative juices flowing – but any lovely book of paintings does the trick.

Inspired to shop

Acquiring fabric is one of the great pleasures of quilting. There's something very lovely about building up a personal collection of fabrics, no matter how modest. Even the smallest pile of delicious-looking patterns and colours will catch your eye when you open the cupboard or walk past the shelf, and suggest interesting combinations and narratives. You only need a few fabrics to start playing and sorting: once you have acquired these, you will soon learn how to recognize your own preferences and tastes, and to see what else is needed to extend or complement your collection.

You may prefer to build up a collection in the traditional thrifty manner, by saving old clothes and bed linen or cutting up summer dresses and cotton shirts, or perhaps you like to barter and swap with friends and fellow quilters. But what if you are new to quilting, or don't have the resources of used or shared fabrics, or simply prefer to buy new fabric for your quilts? In that case, you need to find the best places to shop.

I developed my fabric shopping strategies when I was young and first in love with textiles; I was cash-poor but relatively time-rich and realized that there was enormous fun to be had in spending hours browsing and weighing up options before parting with my hard-earned money. Even now, I don't rush into buying fabric and I don't buy in bulk. In shops I take my time, pile up bolts, make different combinations and look over and over again at the fabrics (it's so easy to overlook gems if you rush).

If I'm shopping online I sit down with a cup of tea, play with wish-lists and design boards, and browse extensively. I then put plenty of fabrics in my basket but leave them there for a day or two before coming back and being ruthlessly selective. Sometimes, though, I simply fall head over heels in love with a fabric, in which case I'm as lost as a Mills & Boon heroine and can only succumb.

The best places to shop are those that offer a good range of fabrics and plenty of inspiration. This may sound obvious, but it's not always that simple. Unless you are able to get to one of the enormous warehouse-style shops in the US that stock a huge number of fabrics, you are limited to the selection made by the owner of a small shop. There are hundreds and hundreds of fabric designs available at any one time, so editing is necessary; if you can find a place where the edited selection matches your tastes, you are in luck. If not, look around and keep trying new places. Or try to get to one of the major quilt shows and festivals, where there are a number of vendors and plenty of choice.

And if you don't have inspirational fabric shops near you (and there is a woeful lack in the UK), the next best option is to buy online. Looking at photographs of little squares of fabric is never the same as seeing and handling the real thing, and there is always an element of risk with colour reproduction and scale of pattern, but the best Internet sellers offer fantastic choice and excellent service. Plus, you are under no obligation to buy, there are no opening and closing times, and you can do your shopping in your pyjamas and dressing gown.

But before you set off to buy:

- It pays to have a look at your collection to remind yourself of what you have already (so you don't end up with a pile of fabrics that all look the same) and what you need.

- If there's a particular quilt in a book or fabric design that has inspired you, take a copy of the book or magazine or the fabric itself to the shop, or keep your source of inspiration next to the computer for easy reference.

- If there's a colour combination you like, take pages from magazines or paint charts to remind you of the exact colours in the shop. Unless you have an amazing memory, it's very easy to forget – or recall incorrectly – and to plump for the wrong shade/ tone. I even bring fabrics to the computer so I can make an educated guess as to what will and won't work.

- I sometimes take a few small cuttings of fabrics I'm planning to use in a quilt or quilts, so that I can check potential matches and thus not waste money. This saves carting bags of fabrics around and is especially useful at big quilt festivals, when it's possible to feel overwhelmed by the choice on offer.

Inspirational blogs and websites

Reading a good craft blog is like a privileged peek into another world — a world of colour, energy, skill and many wonderful creations. If ever you find yourself short of inspiration and enthusiasm, my advice is to visit a few craft blogs for a good dose of cheer and beauty; there is a huge amount of both on beautiful blogs and websites, especially those written and created by fabric and quilt designers. These are the places I visit regularly:

Anna Maria Horner (www.annamariahorner.com)

Amy Butler (www.amybutlerdesign.com)

Heather Ross (www.heatherrossdesigns.com)

Kaffe Fassett (www.kaffefassett.com)

Denyse Schmidt Quilts (www.dsquilts.com)

Posie Gets Cozy (www.posiegetscozy.com)

Purl Bee (www.purlbee.com)

Inspirational collections

There is nothing to beat looking at real quilts for inspiration, and a visit to a museum or gallery can be a path-changing experience. Also, don't overlook private 'collections': you may find that people you know have a few forgotten quilts stored away at the back of a cupboard. Even the most modest of quilts can inspire.

My two favourite public collections are in the American Museum in Britain (www.americanmuseum.org), which is in Bath, and the American Folk Art Museum in New York (www.folkartmuseum.org). More quilts can be seen in the Quilters' Guild Quilt Museum and Gallery in York (www.quiltmuseum.org.uk), the Victoria and Albert Museum in London (www.vam.ac.uk) and the Whitworth Art Gallery in Manchester (www.whitworth.manchester.ac.uk).

Even if you didn't read Lucy Boston's Green Knowe books when you were a child, it is worth getting to the beautiful village of Hemingford Grey to see her patchworks, which are cleverly designed and stitched completely by hand. Make an appointment to see the house and quilts (details on www.greenknowe.co.uk), and you will be amazed. The garden (above) is absolutely beautiful, too, and is looked after by Diana Boston, Lucy Boston's daughter-in-law; try to visit in June, when it is full of roses and irises that may inspire a floral quilt. (The garden is also open through the National Gardens Scheme: www.ngs.org.uk.)

resources

Here are my recommendations for where to buy fabrics and quilting equipment. It is my personal address book and because I buy from places near to me, it is by no means comprehensive. The same applies to the list of websites: these are the ones I like and use all the time.

SHOPS

LONDON

Despite the fact that so many fabric shops and fabric departments have disappeared over the last couple of decades, London is still a great place to buy fabric. I shop centrally, but there are also all sorts of gems in different parts of the city (consult Time Out www.timeout.com). The Soho shops may charge a little more, but I am happy to pay this because the shop assistants are so knowledgeable (many have a fashion/textiles degree and are designers/makers), and the shops are so close to many wonderful cafés. I particularly enjoy browsing in the area around Berwick Street and Broadwick Street.

For quilt fabrics, **Liberty** on Regent Street (**www.liberty.co.uk**) has an excellent selection of Rowan (Westminster) fabrics plus sewing threads and accessories. Many branches of **John Lewis** (**www.johnlewis.com**), both in London and nationwide, carry a selection of patchwork and quilting supplies.

For a large range of natural and beautiful fabrics, including an amazing selection of tie silks:

The Cloth House
47 Berwick Street,
London W1F 8SJ;
and 98 Berwick Street,
London W1F 0QJ.
(**www.clothhouse.com**)

For a lovely range of fabrics and haberdashery:

Ray Stitch
99 Essex Road
London N1 2SJ
(**www.raystitch.co.uk**)

For suiting and shirting:

Textile King
81 Berwick Street,
London W1F 8TW.

For silks and more:
The three following shops are all part of same group
(**www.thesilksociety.com**)

Broadwick Silks
9–11 Broadwick Street,
London W1F 0DB.

The Silk Society
44 Berwick Street,
London W1F 0PP.

The Berwick Street Cloth Shop
14 Berwick Street,
London W1F 8SE.

For unusual fabrics:

Borovick Fabrics
16 Berwick Street,
London W1F 0HP.
(**www.borovickfabricsltd.co.uk**)

OUTSIDE LONDON

Quilters' Haven carries a very good range of fabrics:

Quilters' Haven
68 High Street, Wickham Market,
Suffolk IP13 0QU.
(**www.quilters-haven.co.uk**)

I have not been to the Cotton Patch shop, but their mail-order service is excellent (and they have a large, fabric-filled stand at various quilt fairs):

The Cotton Patch
1283–1285 Stratford Road, Hall Green, Birmingham B28 9AJ.
(**www.cottonpatch.co.uk**)

Tikki Patchwork is a small shop with a lovely range (and is very close to Kew Gardens if you want fabric *and* inspiration):

Tikki Patchwork
293 Sandycombe Lane,
Twickenham TW9 3LU.
(**www.tikkilondon.com**)

OUTSIDE THE UK

I would give my eye teeth to have Purl Patchwork (and its sister, Purl, the yarn shop) right on my doorstep, as it is the most exquisite little shop selling beautifully chosen fabrics. Fortunately, there is a brilliant website and mail-order side to the business, so you don't have to fly all the way to New York to get a serious fabric-fix.

Purl Patchwork
459 Broome Street, New York
NY 10013.
(**www.purlsoho.com**)

WEBSITES

In addition to the websites belonging to the shops mentioned above, I also buy fabric from several Internet-only businesses. Do remember that if you buy from an overseas website, you may be charged extra customs and excise duties as well as a Post Office handling fee (some slip through the net, but you cannot rely on this happening). If you are buying from a US seller, check to see if they offer the standard pre-paid envelope which allows you to buy up to nine yards of fabric for a set rate, as this is the cheapest form of postage. It does mean that you need to calculate your order quite carefully, though.

Glorious Color
(**www.gloriouscolor.com**) is my first stop for fabric designed by Kaffe Fassett and Philip Jacobs (see pages 28 and 136). I've been buying here for years; the website, fabrics and service are all wonderful.

Hawthorne Threads
(**www.hawthornethreads.com**) carries an enormous range of contemporary fabrics by leading designers and manufacturers. It has a fresh, clean style and fabrics to match. The company sells internationally and despatches quickly. It pays to use the flat rate envelope option for international shipping.

Cia's Palette
(**www.ciaspalette.com**) has a great selection of fabrics and offers excellent service.

eBay and **Etsy** both have plenty of members selling fabric for quilting. I found some very good feed sack fabric on **Etsy** (**www.etsy.com**) and an out-of-print fabric on eBay (**www.ebay.co.uk** or **www.ebay.com** in the US).

And finally, the website of **Westminster Fibers** (**www.westminsterfibers.com**), the company that distributes Rowan and Freespirit fabrics. Although they don't sell fabric via the website, it is an excellent resource, as it shows all their fabrics, has details of forthcoming collections, and has links to retailers in the US, many of whom will ship internationally.

Picture credits

1, 2, 3, 4, 5, 9, 24 above left, 25, 26, 33, 34, 35, 36, 39, 43, 44–45, 51, 59, 61, 62, 73, 78, 79, 85, 91, 97, 98, 105, 106, 113, 115, 117, 121, 127, 133: Kristin Perers

11: John Sharman, *At the End of the Porch*, c.1918 (oil on canvas)/ Indianapolis Museum of Art, U.S.A./James E. Roberts Fund/Bridgeman Art Library; 56 above left: Getty Images/ Martin Child; 56 below right: Getty Images/ Gavin Hellier;

56 below left: Getty Images/ Harald Sund; 56 above right: Boris Mikhailovich Kustodiev, *Merchant's woman with a mirror* (oil on canvas)/State Russian Museum, St. Petersburg, Russia/ Bridgeman Art Library; 82 right, 88 above right and below left: Getty Images; 110 below left: GAP Photos/ Marcus Harpur; 106 above left and right: GAP Photos/Zara Napier; 110 below right: GAP Photos/Richard Bloom; 124 above left: GAP Photos/ Mark Bolton;

124 below right: GAP Photos/ Friedrich Strauss; 130: Sir Walter Russell, *The Morning Room*, c.1907 (oil on canvas)/Leeds Museums and Galleries, U.K./Bridgeman Art Library/Getty Images. 147–151: Geoff Dann

All other photography by Jane Brocket.

Illustrations by Trina Dalziel.

acknowledgements

Writing this book has been a truly enjoyable experience, made all the more so by the people who have contributed in some way.

I would like to thank the team at Pavilion, especially Katie Cowan for giving me the chance to do something I love on a grand scale, and Miriam Hyslop for her vision, high standards and exemplary project management. Many thanks, too, to Kristin Perers for her wonderful, luminous photographs and to Alex Lewis for his impeccable styling. I am grateful to Paul Tilby for the book's lovely look and design, to Trina Dalziel for her beautiful illustrations, and to Fiona Corbridge for her careful editorial work.

This book could not have been written without a large amount of inspiration, and for this I would like to thank some very special creative people who have inspired me to quilt. They are Kaffe Fassett, Brandon Mably, Liza Prior Lucy, Marilyn Phipps, Linda Miller, Julie Arkell and Janet Bolton.

I have been fortunate to have the encouragement and support of some very thoughtful and helpful people; many thanks to Stephen Sheard of Rowan, Kay Gardiner, Alicia Paulson, Marion Farrell, Lucy Weston-Webb, Angela Burdett and to the many readers of my blog, Yarnstorm, all of whom have been simply brilliant. Susie Green of Duxhurst Quilting not only has a fine eye for backing fabrics, but she has also been a tremendous source of practical advice and help, and I would like to say a special thank you to her. My agent Jane Graham Maw also deserves another huge vote of thanks for her calm guidance and constant support.

I bought the majority of the fabrics to make the quilts in this book, but I am grateful to Westminster Fibers for the boxful of beautiful fabrics that they kindly sent to me.

Making a large number of quilts in a relatively short space of time has placed a few unusual demands upon my family, but they have come up trumps in terms of patience and advice. I thank Tom for his excellent colour and design sense, Phoebe for her textile enthusiasm, and Alice for looking so lovely wrapped in quilts. And I must thank my husband, Simon, not only for saying 'That's nice' every time there was a quilt blocking his path, but also for being my rock-solid rock.

Jane Brocket